KING

To be r

—4. DEC

19

Methuen Playscripts

The Methuen Playscripts series exists
to extend the range of plays in print by
publishing work which is not yet widely
known but which has already earned a
place in the acting repertoire of the
modern theatre.

The Idiot

Simon Gray's dramatization of The Idiot was first
presented by the National Theatre at the Old Vic
in the summer of 1970. In creating a stage play
based upon Dostoievsky's original novel, the
playwright has taken some of the most vivid and
contrasting episodes recounting the strange in-
volvement between Prince Myshkin, the good
natured 'Idiot', the beautiful Nastasya Filippovna
and her desperate lover and husband, Rogozhin.
The ambiguity of these episodes and the para-
doxical atmosphere of Dostoievsky's novel –
hovering between sombre tragedy and grotesque
farce – is heightened by the use of a strange,
sinister commentator, the character Ferdyschenko.
The result is a haunting piece of theatrical
bravura, oddly and unexpectedly true to the
spirit of the original book.

By the same author

Sleeping Dog
Wise Child
Dutch Uncle
Spoiled

Other Methuen Playscripts

Paul Ableman	TESTS
	BLUE COMEDY
Barry Bermange	NATHAN AND TABILETH
	and OLDENBURG
John Bowen	THE CORSICAN BROTHERS
Howard Brenton	REVENGE
	CHRISTIE IN LOVE and other plays
Henry Chapman	YOU WON'T ALWAYS BE ON TOP
Peter Cheeseman	THE KNOTTY
David Cregan	THREE MEN FOR COLVERTON
	TRANSCENDING and THE DANCERS
	THE HOUSES BY THE GREEN
	MINIATURES
Rosalyn Drexler	THE INVESTIGATION and HOT BUTTERED ROLL
Harrison, Melfi, Howard	NEW SHORT PLAYS
Duffy, Harrison, Owens	NEW SHORT PLAYS: 2
Henry Livings	GOOD GRIEF!
	THE LITTLE MRS FOSTER SHOW
	HONOUR AND OFFER
	PONGO PLAYS 1-6
John McGrath	EVENTS WHILE GUARDING THE BOFORS GUN
David Mercer	THE GOVERNOR'S LADY
Georges Michel	THE SUNDAY WALK
Rodney Milgate	A REFINED LOOK AT EXISTENCE
Guillaume Oyono-Mbia	THREE SUITORS: ONE HUSBAND and UNTIL FURTHER NOTICE
Alan Plater	CLOSE THE COALHOUSE DOOR
David Selbourne	THE PLAY OF WILLIAM COOPER AND EDMUND DEW-NEVETT
	THE TWO-BACKED BEAST
	DORABELLA
Johnny Speight	IF THERE WEREN'T ANY BLACKS YOU'D HAVE TO INVENT THEM
Martin Sperr	TALES FROM LANDSHUT
Boris Vian	THE KNACKER'S ABC
Lanford Wilson	HOME FREE! and THE MADNESS OF LADY BRIGHT

The Idiot

SIMON GRAY

adapted from
the novel by
Fyodor Dostoievsky

First published in 1971 by
Methuen & Co Ltd
11 New Fetter Lane, London EC4
Copyright © 1971 by Simon Gray

Reproduced and Printed in Great Britain by
Redwood Press Limited, Trowbridge & London

Principal Characters

PARFYON ROGOZHIN A short man of about twenty-seven with curly hair, almost black and tiny but fiery eyes. Nose broad and flat, thin lips continually curled into a sort of insolent, sarcastic and even malicious smile, but forehead high and well-shaped. Face deathly pale.

PRINCE MYSHKIN About twenty-seven, slighly above medium height, with very thick, fair hair, hollow cheeks, and a thin pointed and almost white little beard. Eyes large, blue and piercing with something gentle but heavy in their look; face pleasant, sensitive and lean, though colourless.

LEBEDEV About forty, of strong build, with a red nose and pimply face.

GAVRILA IVOLGIN (GANYA) Very good looking, about twenty-eight. Slender, fair-haired, with a small imperial, and an intelligent and handsome face. His smile amiable but too exquisite, revealing a row of altogether too dazzling teeth; in spite of his gaiety and good nature, the look in his eyes is a little too intent and searching.

GENERAL YEPANCHIN Fifty-six, fine complexion, excellent health, stocky, solid figure.

MRS YEPANCHIN Middle fifties, a tall spare woman, aquiline nose, hollow, sallow cheeks and thick sunken lips. A high but narrow forehead, rather large grey eyes which sometimes have a most unexpected expression. Eccentric.

ADELAIDA YEPANCHIN Beautiful, rather sad face. Reminds Myshkin of Holbein's Madonna in Dresden. Age twenty-five. She is the eldest daughter, easy to get on with.

AGLAYA YEPANCHIN The youngest, most beautiful and gifted daughter. Temperamental and charming.

NASTASYA FILIPPOVNA Extraordinarily beautiful. Dark hair and eyes. Thin, pensive face, haughty and passionate expression.

TOTSKY Fifty-five. Wealthy, moves in high society. Extraordinarily artistic tastes and exceptional egotism.

FERDYSCHENKO About thirty, tall and broad-shouldered with
a huge curly ginger head. Face red and fleshy, lips thick, nose
broad and flat, eyes tiny and lost in fat, seems to be winking
all the time. Rather insolent, dirty clothes.

RADOMSKY Twenty-eight, tall and slim. Handsome and intelligent. Large eyes, witty and ironic.

KELLER 'Retired Lieutenant.' Ex-pugilist, age thirty.

ANTIP BURDOVSKY Twenty-two, poorly and slovenly dressed
with an innocently insolent look. Speaks agitatedly and stam-
meringly.

IPPOLIT TERENTYEV Seventeen or eighteen with an intelligent
but irritable expression. Looks in the last stages of consumption,
thin as a rake, pale and yellow, with glittering eyes and two
hectic spots on his cheeks.

SOME OTHER CHARACTERS

PRINCESS BELEKONSKY

ELDER STATESMAN

PETROVICH

PRINCE SHULOVSKY

The Idiot was first presented by the National Theatre Company at the Old Vic on July 15 1970 with the following cast:

FERDYSCHENKO	David Ryall
PRINCE LEO NIKOLAIEVISH MYSHKIN	Derek Jacobi
PARFYON ROGOZHIN	Tom Baker
LEBEDEV	Edward Hardwicke
TOTSKY	Kenneth Mackintosh
GENERAL YEPANCHIN	Michael Turner
MRS YEPANCHIN	Hazel Hughes
ALEXANDRA YEPANCHIN	Judy Wilson
ADELAIDA YEPANCHIN	Maggie Riley
AGLAYA YEPANCHIN	Louise Purnell
ROGOZHIN'S FOLLOWERS	Alan Dudley
	Michael Edgar
	Tom Georgeson
	Barry James
	Lewis Jones
	David Henry
	Malcolm Reid
KELLER	John Flint
MONEYLENDER	James Fagan
GANYA IVOLGIN	Frank Barrie
NASTASYA FILIPPOVNA	Gillian Barge
PRINCE SHULOVSKY	Richard Kay
RADOMSKY	Benjamin Whitrow
IPPOLIT	Ronald Pickup
BURDOVSKY	Michael Tudor Barnes
PRINCESS BELEKONSKY	Mary Griffiths
ELDER STATESMAN	Harry Lomax
GENERAL PETROVICH	Anthony Nicholls
ACCORDIONIST	Henry Krein
GUITARIST	Rod Willmott

Produced by Anthony Quayle and settings by Josef Svoboda.

The action takes place in St Petersburg and Pavlovsk in the late 1860s.

ACT ONE

Scene One

The bar.

TWO MEN are sitting at the bar table.

Others are singing softly, clapping their hands, offstage.

FERDYSCHENKO sits drinking occasionally, clapping his hands to the music and laughing.

A MAN drinking at the table next to FERDYSCHENKO, and with a half-full bottle, gets up and goes to the lavatory. FERDY-SCHENKO fills his glass from the man's bottle. The other MAN looks at his bottle, then glares, fixes his gaze on FERDY-SCHENKO, who toasts him blandly.

All this before the lights go down on the audience.

Then just as the lights go down, the MAN on the other side of FERDYSCHENKO gets up to go and FERDYSCHENKO attempts the same trick. The FIRST MAN sees him, comes over, grabs FERDYSCHENKO by the collar, shakes him. The song and the clapping go on through this.

Lights go down on the audience.

MAN: Who are you anyway, you damned thief?

    (Exit into bar.)

FERDYSCHENKO: Ferdyschenko, sir, and you're quite right, a
    thief and a coward. Forgive me, sir.

    (FERDYSCHENKO laughs, throws out his arms.)

    And a <u>Russian!</u> Ferdeschenko. Fer-dee-schenko, the Russian.
    In which case, a walking paradox, a profane embodiment of
    the great creative spirit, <u>a swine of God!</u> Eh? Listen, if I
    stink it's only because my poor soul's on flower. When I'm
    drunk, it's to dream of Christ, his passion, and my re-
    demption, and I laugh in hol-y blasphemy, as the saints
    do weep with joy. All of which is to say - I am a Russian!
    Look at me and you look on every compartment in this
    vast land -

    (As with a hoot and a whistle the compartment containing
    MYSHKIN rocks on stage.)

- every peasant, every saint, every mortal traveller - haaah, there! See what I mean?

(As MYSHKIN's compartment is lit up. MYSHKIN is sitting staring straight ahead. ROGOZHIN, not as yet properly distinct, is lying across the seat, his head on MYSHKIN's knees.)

See - there - that's a Russian face, and an exceptionally noble face, the face of an aristocrat and a saint. What a sweet expression, eh? And what a delightful smile?

(As MYSHKIN smiles.)

Oh, there's love there all right, so there's Russia there all right. The only thing - can you see it? Here? The mouth?

(Touching his own mouth.)

Isn't there something a bit funny - no, it's the lower jaw -

(Waggles his own lower jaw.)

- yes, a distinct touch of slackness - something not quite - mmmm? Something just a little - mmm - missing? Ah-hah, but not missing any longer. That's a Russian face, too eh? Oh, that's the face for me.

(ROGOZHIN rears suddenly up, glares ferociously and be-wildered at MYSHKIN, moves away from him and rubbing at his face, stares at MYSHKIN, who smiles back at him, as.)

RAILWAY GUARD: St Petersburg half an hour. St Petersburg half an hour.

Scene Two

The Train

ROGOZHIN (to MYSHKIN): You're cold.

(MYSHKIN looks towards him, smiles, nods.)

I fell asleep on top of you?

MYSHKIN: Yes, you fell, you see. I didn't want to disturb you. I hope you don't mind.

ROGOZHIN (laughs): Mind? Why should I mind? You're nice

and soft, eh?

(Pause.)

Been abroad?

MYSHKIN: Yes, I've been in Switzerland. For many years.

ROGOZHIN: Switzerland? People only go to Switzerland when they're ill.

MYSHKIN: I've been suffering from a nervous disorder. Well, really a kind of... it was my brain.

ROGOZHIN (laughs. MYSHKIN joining in): Nervous? Idiocy? What – twitchings and jerkings and fainting fits, eh? Cured you, did they?

MYSHKIN: Well, I'm not quite cured, but I'm much better. I haven't had an attack for a long time.

ROGOZHIN: Not even when you saw the bill? They live off Russians, the Swiss do. It's when you're broke that they say you're cured. And you're broke, aren't you? Eh? I bet that's why they let you out.

MYSHKIN: No, they were very nice to me, although it's true I haven't got any money at the moment, although I've got a letter somewhere –

(Begins vaguely to search for it.)

– my parents are dead, you see – they died when I was very young – but a friend of the family – Mr Pavlischev – he became my guardian. When I became ill he paid my fees. Mr Pavlischev was a good man – a great man – but now – well, anyway, I'm going to St Petersburg to see some relatives and I've got this letter –

ROGOZHIN: That little bundle there, is that your possessions?

MYSHKIN: Yes. Well, until I um, see about –

ROGOZHIN: You've got a good face, haven't you? A good face!

(Laughs.)

A holy face. Perhaps you're a holy idiot, eh? What's your name?

MYSHKIN: Myshkin. Leo Nikolaievich, the Prince Myshkin.

ROGOZHIN: A Prince? What, a real Prince, are you?

MYSHKIN: Yes, a real Prince. I'm a real Prince.

ROGOZHIN: Well, Prince, ever heard the name Rogozhin? Do you know that name?

MYSHKIN (as LEBEDEV's head appears above the seat behind MYSHKIN's and ROGOZHIN's head): Rogo - um, no, I'm afraid - Rogo - ?

ROGOZHIN: Rogozhin.

LEBEDEV: Not Parfyon Rohozhin, son of Simeon, recently deceased? (Raptly.)

ROZOGHIN (looks at LEBEDEV, laughs contemptuously): He knows me, you see.

LEBEDEV: Just come into a fortune estimated at a million and twelve hundred roubles, oh, I know you, sir, I don't know you, Prince whatever-it-is you claim to be -

MYSHKIN: Um, Myshkin. Leo Nikol -

LEBEDEV: - but I know you, sir.

(Comes around into the compartment.)

Lebedev, my lord. Lebedev, and oh, the privilege -

(ROGOZHIN shoves LEBEDEV to the floor.)

(On the floor.) Oh, sir, thank you, sir, beat me and I'm yours. Oh I know you, my lord!

ROGOZHIN: Do you? What else do you know, besides my name? Eh?

(Prods him with his toe.)

LEBEDEV: Why, I know the name of - of a lady, sir. I know the name of a lady.

(Tries to sit between MYSHKIN and ROGOZHIN. ROGOZHIN kicks at him, he slides adroitly out of reach.)

I do, sir, thank you, sir, yes, the name of the lady for whose sake his father -

(To MYSHKIN.)

- tried to beat him to death with a stick and drove him out of the country when he failed. Beat him - his own father -

(To ROGOZHIN.)

- and are you quite recovered, sir? You look feverish. Keep that chest warm, I beg you! Yes, his own father hounded him out of the country and then - then - oh, most Holy Lord, oh the sheer justice of it - this same father - before he could so much as change his will - dropped dead. And - and left this royal young Rogozhin a fortune! Yeah! a fortune! For which I devour you with admiration and give thanks and Hossannahs on my knees. Oh, I know all about the lady you suffered for, sir,

(Dodges about the kick.)

Thank you, sir.

ROGOZHIN: Do you? Do you?

(Kicking at LEBEDEV, who replies automatically with 'thank yous' while attempting to dodge the kicks.)

Do you? Hah - two weeks ago I was famous because I was a thief, Prince. Now -

(Gestures to LEBEDEV.)

LEBEDEV: Oh, not a thief, never a thief - why, he merely purloined some of his father's bonds to buy ear-rings for the lady. Thank you, sir! But think - think - if you hadn't stolen, my lord, your father wouldn't have killed himself trying to beat you to death, and then you wouldn't have inherited his money. Out of evil cometh good! Wonderous are His ways!

ROGOZHIN: Shut up!

(Turns, looks at MYSHKIN.)

Well, Prince - well, Prince of the Holy Face, well - what do you think of me, eh? What do you think of a man who'd do a thing like that, eh?

MYSHKIN: I - I -

(Shakes his head.)

ROGOZHIN (peers at him): Here, yes, a Holy Face, it is a Holy Face, a face loved by God, that's what it is, eh?

LEBEDEV: And such Christ loveth.

ROGOZHIN: Well, go on, Prince, you tell me what you think. I want to know what a man like you thinks of a man like me.

MYSHKIN: I - I don't know anything about women, but I think you must love her very much.

ROGOZHIN: Love her! Love her! She's my life. My life!

MYSHKIN: And that story about the ear-rings, I think that what you did for the ear-rings, that was a beautiful thing to do, beautiful.

ROGOZHIN: Ah, but not as beautiful as what I'm going to do when we get to St Petersburg, Prince. I'm going to marry her! Yes, marry her! I'm a rich man now, and I'm going to marry her.

LEBEDEV (sitting up again behind ROGOZHIN, in the next compartment): No, sir, I'm afraid that's out of the question, sir - you're too late -

ROGOZHIN: What? What do you say? What do you say?

(Seizing him by the collar over the seat.)

LEBEDEV: But didn't you know, sir, the rumour's all over St Petersburg. Totsky's going to marry her off. She's going to be married off. Totsky's finding her a husband.

ROGOZHIN: Totsky! Totsky! Tell me - tell me.

LEBEDEV: Why, Nastasya Filippovna's been Totsky's woman since she was a little girl, and now he's tired of her and he's planned to get rid of her in marriage.

(ROGOZHIN rises menacingly over LEBEDEV pulling at his scarf.)

ROGOZHIN: Now! Now you tell me! You tell me everything!

(Lights go down on the train.)

FERDYSCHENKO: Yes, that sounds like trouble for someone.

(He laughs, then raises his voice to a bellow.)

But don't let that put you off, ladies and gentlemen... it's still the auction of the season! And Lebedev's right - it's begun -

Scene Three

The YEPANCHIN living-room

As lights go up on the YEPANCHIN living-room, TOTSKY and YEPANCHIN. TOTSKY is carrying a flat package, YEPANCHIN is peering furtively at TOTSKY as TOTSKY begins to unwrap the package.

FERDYSCHENKO: There! On the left! The proud owner and vendor – and on the right – his friend and procurer – two gentlemen who know a gorgeous filly when they see it – and – there she is – there she is – ladies and gentlemen – the bargain of St Petersburg –

(As the picture of NASTASYA is taken out, TOTSKY holds it up, YEPANCHIN steps back to scrutinize it.)

Nast-asya Filippovna, this marvellous mount! For sale! What are we bid!

YEPANCHIN: Fifty roubles?

TOTSKY: Fifty roubles.

YEPANCHIN: A bargain. An absolute bargain! I must get him to do my wife. Here.

(Takes the picture from YEPANCHIN, holds it up for TOTSKY.)

TOTSKY: My dear fellow –

(Shudders, looks at the picture sideways on and almost surreptitiously.)

Mm! You know what he's caught, damn him! He's caught that thing – lunacy – in her eyes – that time she came at me with a paper-knife.

(Little pause, laughs.)

Mais quelle créature magnifique, eh?

(Seems suddenly to be held by the picture, then goes over, takes it firmly from YEPANCHIN.)

No, I couldn't sleep with that in the house. Come to that, I couldn't with the original for one reason or another.

(Puts the picture on the table.)

Perhaps you'd better go and get our young – then?

YEPANCHIN (nervously): I hope he's calmer than –

(Goes to the door, looks back at TOTSKY, then goes off.)

(TOTSKY stands in the centre of the room, makes as if to look at the picture, then walks away.)

FERDYSCHENKO: You see how reluctantly he's giving her up! Oh, it wasn't an easy choice, a wild, wonderful mount like that!

(As TOTSKY goes back to the picture, looks down at it, turns his head away.)

What's he going to do for his exercise now!

(As TOTSKY bends over the picture again, and simultaneously.

ADÉLAIDA comes in.)

ADELAIDA: Oh.

(Standing at the door.)

TOTSKY (turns, stares at her, smiles, pushes the picture away behind him): Miss Adelaida - Adelaida!

(Goes over to her, takes her hand, smiles into her eyes, raises her hand to her lips.)

Were you looking for your papa?

ADELAIDA: I'm to ask -

(Demurely smiling.)

If you're joining us for lunch.

TOTSKY: For lunch?

(Still smiling into her eyes.)

Well, ·your papa and I have something particular - very particular - to discuss. But afterwards I hope I shall have the right - and the honour - of talking to you. Eh?

ADELAIDA (in confusion): I'll tell mama.

(Does a bashful curtsey and goes out.

TOTSKY smiling at the door.)

FERDYSCHENKO: Ah! You see - this isn't a cattle market! This is a St Petersburg living-room, where they're up to thinking and speaking in -

TOTSKY: Ça, c'est une jeune fille très propre et très jolie!

(Simultaneously YEPANCHIN comes in with his arm around GANYA.

TOTSKY smoothly picks up the picture, shows it to GANYA.)

My dear, Ganya!

YEPANCHIN (with false eagerness): Well?

GANYA: And what am I to do with that?

YEPANCHIN: Why, um, cherish it, old chap.

TOTSKY: Virtually a betrothal gift.

GANYA: So my betrothal gift from my bride to be –

(Calmly smiling.)

– is a picture of herself paid for by her guardian.

FERDYSCHENKO: Oh, quel esprit de géometrie!

(Into the silence, as YEPANCHIN and TOTSKY are exchanging looks.)

YEPANCHIN (reproachfully): Ganya! Mr Totsky was only –

(Interrupted by a crash from outside the main door.)

TOTSKY: Good God!

YEPANCHIN: What on earth –

(Goes over to the door.)

Sergei! Sergei! What's going on?

FERDYSCHENKO: It's a Russian, sir! Come to slaughter the French!

SERGEI (muttering to YEPANCHIN, just outside the door): It's a um, gentleman, sir.

(His voice drowned out by FERDYSCHENKO.)

Claims to be related to your wife, sir. He's just knocked over a vase – says he's a Prince Myshkin, sir...

FERDYSCHENKO (bellowing, drowning out SERGEI and YEPAN-CHIN): Kill them, kill them, Rogozhin! Kill! Kill! Kill!

YEPANCHIN: Well, um, um –

(At a loss.)

You'd better show him in, I suppose.

(SERGEI goes out.)

Most extraordinary!

(Going to GANYA.)

There's some um, lunatic outside knocking over our vases and claiming to be –

(Turns towards the door as SERGEI reappears.)

MYSHKIN: Please forgive me!

(To SERGEI, fails to see a chair, which he nearly knocks over.)

FERDYSCHENKO: Oh, Christ!

YEPANCHIN: Um, Prince Myshkin, is it?

MYSHKIN (nods, smiling): I'm - I'm dreadfully sorry about the vase. My elbow -

(Touches it.)

- your footman - Sergei, isn't it? - was so kind -

YEPANCHIN: Well, I'm glad to hear it.

(Staring at him.)

And you, um, claim to be a relative of my - um wife's?

MYSHKIN: I wrote you a letter...

GANYA: That's right, General. The letter - if you remember -

(Pointedly.)

- was from Switzerland. A Clinic for Nervous Disorders. I passed it on but -

(Maliciously.)

- perhaps you haven't had a chance to read it?

TOTSKY: A Clinic for - ?

MYSHKIN: Yes. You probably haven't heard of me before, I - you see, I've been ill for a very long time - with a - there was something wrong with my brain, I had terrible attacks, in fact -

(Laughs.)

- I was almost an idiot.

YEPANCHIN: Indeed?

(Apprehensively, takes a step back.)

MYSHKIN: Oh, I'm quite well now, I haven't had an attack for a long time.

(Laughs.)

YEPANCHIN: Oh - oh good.

MYSHKIN: Yes, it is, isn't it? And it's so wonderful to be home again.

YEPANCHIN: Home?

MYSHKIN (laughs): Oh, in Russia, I mean. You see, General, your wife is the only relative I have. My guardian died just two weeks ago –

(Begins to fumble into his bundle.)

I'm not very good at understanding business letters – it's one of the reasons I took the liberty.

(Looks at their faces.)

It is a liberty, isn't it? I see that now.

(Shoves the letter back into his pocket.)

Please forgive me, I've got so much to learn about, um, how to do things with people.

(Turns to the door.)

YEPANCHIN: No, no, look here, we're not sending you away, you know. You mustn't think that. Mrs Yepanchin –

(Drawing him back by the arm.)

– would never forgive me if I sent away one of her relatives.

TOTSKY: I say, did you really arrive here in those clothes? In this weather?

MYSHKIN: Yes. I'm sorry. They're all I have at the moment.

TOTSKY: What about money? Have you got any?

MYSHKIN: Well, no, but, you see, this letter, um.

(Begins to search again.)

TOTSKY: But if you haven't got any money, how did you pay for your treatment in Switzerland?

MYSHKIN: Oh, well, my parents died when I was very young but a friend of the family – a Mr Pavilschev – he became my guardian. He looked after me, and paid all my bills at the clinic.

TOTSKY: Did he? That was very civil of him.

(Sceptically.)

MYSHKIN: Oh yes, my guardian – Mr Pavilschev was a great

man - a very good man - almost a saint. He died two weeks ago. And as the solicitors told me -

(To YEPANCHIN.)

- that Mrs Yepanchin was my only relative -

TOTSKY: They told you to try your luck with the General?

MYSHKIN: Luck?

(Confused.)

Um, this letter -

(Begins to search again.)

YEPANCHIN: Do you know, sir, I believe you're an honest man, sir.

(As if surprised at himself.)

In fact, Prince, I trust you completely. There.

(Shakes hands.)

MYSHKIN (laughs): Oh, I've been telling you the truth. But thank you for believing me.

YEPANCHIN: But if you are - as you are honest, it makes it rather - I mean, you see, you're a member of the family, so to speak - and you're, well - we can't have that, can we? Your um, circumstances, I mean.

TOTSKY (laughs): Especially as you're honest - that won't improve your circumstances, you know - not in St Petersburg.

GANYA: I have an idea, sir.

(Maliciously.)

You'll be needing someone to replace me after all and -

YEPANCHIN: Well, really, the Prince -

(Laughs.)

GANYA: But why not? I leave to take up your post -

(To TOTSKY.)

- so to speak and a Prince immediately appears to take up mine.

YEPANCHIN: Ganya Ivolgin, my secretary.

GANYA: How do you do? Look, I'll tell you what -

(Takes MYSHKIN's arm, leads him to the desk, moves MYSHKIN's bundle which is on top of the picture of NAS-TASYA, he picks it up.)

- give us a sample of your handwriting. That was the only test I had to take. Here -

MYSHKIN: Oh! Look.

(Stares at the picture, shocked.)

But it's - it's beautiful. She's beautiful!

GANYA: Many people have said so. May I - ?

(Makes to move it out of the way.)

MYSHKIN: Please! May I ask who it is?

(There is a silence.)

YEPANCHIN: That is the young lady that Ganya is going to marry. Nastasya Filippovna.

MYSHKIN: Nastasya Filippovna!

YEPANCHIN (surprised): Yes, sir. Mr Totsky's ward.

MYSHKIN: Mr Totsky!
(Looks at TOTSKY.)

TOTSKY: Sir!

MYSHKIN: And it's you who - Nastasya Filippovna is your -

YEPANCHIN (as MYSHKIN goes on staring at TOTSKY): Mr Totsky has um raised Nastasya Filippovan since she was a child, a homeless child - a very sad story, as you can imagine - the little orphan - but now - well, a happy, a most happy conclusion, eh, Ganya?

MYSHKIN: Yes, yes, I've heard about you and your ward, Mr Totsky.

GANYA: Oh, did you? Where?

MYSHKIN (attempting to say): On the train from -

GANYA (ignoring him): So my bride to be is the gossip of Swiss lunatic asylums, is she? Perhaps -

(To MYSHKIN.)

- you'd like to make her a donation - people do like to, you know - chance acquaintances or people who've heard of her by reputation - a pair of ear-rings from a mad thief for instance - a necklace -

(Laughs.)

- did you know she had a new necklace -

(Turning on YEPANCHIN and TOTSKY.)

- she won't say who it came from - but it wasn't from Rogozhin presumably, she only permits herself one scandal with each gift...

(Voice rising hysterically.)

YEPANCHIN: Ganya.

(Takes his arm.)

I'm very sorry, Prince, a small domestic um...

TOTSKY: There's no need to worry about -

(Gestures.)

- Rogozhin - his father's hounded him to the other side of Russia. Poor fellow's probably rotting in a gutter.

(Chuckles comfortingly.)

MYSHKIN: Excuse me, no, he's here, in St Petersburg.

(Pause.)

I met him on the train, you see. It was he that told me about Nastasya Filippovna.

GANYA (after a pause): Indeed. And what, exactly, did he tell you?

MYSHKIN: Well -

(Embarrassed.)

- that he'd come back to marry her.

YEPANCHIN (after another pause, laughs): Fellow hasn't got a rouble to his name.

(He and TOTSKY laugh again, look reassuringly at GANYA.)

MYSHKIN: No, excuse me, I believe he has one and a half million roubles, he told me. His father's just died, you see, and left him all his -

GANYA: Splendid. That's splendid.

(Turns, walks out.)

TOTSKY (exchanging a glance with YEPANCHIN): That damned
Rogozhin –

MYSHKIN (suddenly breaking out): But he mustn't marry her!
He mustn't!

TOTSKY: What?

(Laughs.)

Rogozhin? I don't think there's –

MYSHKIN (shaking his head): No, Ganya – Mr Ivolgin – he
mustn't either.

(Little pause.)

Must he?

TOTSKY: What the devil do you mean? He wants to marry her.

MYSHKIN: No, no – but her – Nastasya Filippovna – look, she's
so beautiful.

TOTSKY: Not generally considered a disadvantage in a bride.

MYSHKIN: But it's the unhappiness, don't you see. Her eyes – do
you see? Look – she mustn't be made to do this, must she?

TOTSKY: What?

(Infuriated.)

Who the Hell do you think you are, coming in here from
some – some –

(YEPANCHIN turns to MYSHKIN.)

YEPANCHIN: I think perhaps, Prince –

(Takes his arm.)

– you're a little over-wrought after your journey, I'm sure
you could do with a bite, eh?

(Leading him across the room to the door, he ushers
MYSHKIN out of the door. MYSHKIN having removed the
picture accidentally returns with the picture to give it back
to YEPANCHIN then exits.)

Sergei – Sergei take the Prince down to Mrs Yepanchin –
eh?

(Comes back, puts his finger to his head, taps it.)

A little bit –

TOTSKY: Stark raving mad!

(Still furious.)

Absolutely lunatic! I've never heard such impertinence in my life.

(Pulls himself together.)

But look here – that Ganya – do you think he's going to back out? Eh? I have to get rid of Nastasya, you know. Everything depends on it... my marriage to your daughter...

YEPANCHIN: No, no, of course not. He wants the dowry, you see. I know Ganya, he might kick up a bit, but he'll stick it out.

TOTSKY: But still – that ruffian Rogozhin coming back to make trouble. Do you think he sent her the necklace – I've seen it too, you know – somebody gave it to her all right.

(FERDYSCHENKO laughing.)

YEPANCHIN: Oh –

(Flustered.)

– perhaps she bought it herself, some perfectly simple explanation, or an old friend, eh?

(FERDYSCHENKO laughs.)

but as for Rogozhin.

(As he speaks lights have gone up in the bar behind FERDYSCHENKO, showing ROGOZHIN surrounded by loungers, louts, etc; trying on a hat in a mirror, held up for him by one of the louts.)

TOTSKY: The fellow's a lout. Nastasya'll soon put him in his place.

Scene Four

The Bar

ROGUES: Here's Keller – Keller.

(Laughs, etc; shouts, as KELLER enters, carrying a small package, opens it, hands a knife to ROGOZHIN.)

ROGOZHIN: Aaaah!

 (Takes the knife from him.)

ROGUES: Kill him, kill, kill, kill, kill, ahh, etc.

ROGOZHIN (as GANYA comes into the room): They'll marry her off to a corpse! A corpse!

 (Raises the knife slowly to his lips, kisses it, almost as a ritual.

 Whilst in the Yepanchin living-room.)

YEPANCHIN: Now, Ganya, there's nothing at all to worry about. We can promise you that.

TOTSKY: You're allowing your imagination to get over-heated, that's all.

 (Back at the bar, ROGOZHIN, completing the kiss, raises the knife above his head, as.)

ROGUES (while ROGOZHIN raises the knife): Kill him, kill him, kill him.

ROGOZHIN: Shut up! Shut up! This is for him! Find out who he is, and let me give him this! And you! You! Get me a money lender. Get me money for her.

 (Bundles LEBEDEV out of the room, following, amidst shouts, etc.)

FERDYSCHENKO (laughing): Well, that's Ganya's future settled, eh?

 (As lights dim on the living-room, TOTSKY and YEPANCHIN having exited.)

 With so many people interested in it too, lucky youth.

 (Rubs his hands.)

 But what about our Prince, come among sophisticates? How is he dealing with the ladies of the Yepanchin Household? With charm, with elegance, with lively conversation.

Scene Five

YEPANCHIN Dining-room

Lights go up.

MYSHKIN brays like a donkey.

AGLAYA laughs at him, contemptuously.

MRS YEPANCHIN, ADELAIDA, ALEXANDRIA, AGLAYA and
MYSHKIN are sitting at a table. GANYA remains, seated,
writing at the desk.

MRS YEPANCHIN: Why are you laughing, Aglaya? One of you
    two ninnies will certainly end up married to one - besides
    the Prince's donkey was exceptional, wasn't it, Prince?

MYSHKIN: Well, no, I don't think so. I just liked the noise it
    made - it is such a hopeful sound, isn't it, you see. Eeeeaw,
    eeeeaw. Besides donkeys are such useful, good-natured
    creatures -

AGLAYA: But can't you tell us about your <u>interesting</u> experiences.

MRS YEPANCHIN: Yes, Prince, come along, Prince.

MYSHKIN (thinks): Well, I don't know if it's interesting. I hope
    it is - but recently I met a man who was sentenced to death
    and then reprieved. He was taken out and actually tied to
    a post and he thought he only had about - five minutes to
    live.

MRS YEPANCHIN (after a pause): Well - tell us - was he
    frightened?

MYSHKING: Oh no - he was quite calm, he said. Anyway at first,
    in fact, he'd never felt so calm in his life - you see there
    was a church nearby, and he - um, he began to stare at it,
    he said, at its roof, the sun was flashing off it, it was - it
    was - he couldn't move his eyes from the sun flashing, and
    he was thinking, well, in two minutes, in one minute I'll
    be dead and - he thought how beautiful the sun was, and
    this was like - he said it was like the beginning of life, and
    he thought, 'What if I had more time to live? Another week
    even - why that would be an eternity.' And as he stood
    there waiting to be shot he was filled with such despair,
    such anger, such bitterness that he prayed to be killed as
    fast as God could arrange it.

(In the Yepanchin living-room, GANYA crumples a letter

he has been trying to write.)

AGLAYA (after a dramatic pause): Yes? And what's the point of this anecdote, please? I'm sure you mean it to have some moral or other.

MYSHKIN: Oh, none, I'm sorry - except -

(Smiling.)

- it must have been so terrible, so terrible.

(Pause.)

I just remembered the man -

ADELAIDA: But he was reprieved?

MYSHKIN: Yes. Yes, he was.

AGLAYA: But there is a moral, you see. It's just that the Prince is too shy to draw it to our attention.

MRS YEPANCHIN: Aglaya - you will not be rude.

(Little pause.)

What moral?

AGLAYA: Go on, Prince - tell us what he did with the eternity he got with his reprieve.

MYSHKIN: Oh - oh, nothing in particular, I'm afraid. He was really, well, just like everybody else.

MRS YEPANCHIN: There you are! Everything's simple if you're going to be shot - but the rest of us have to behave as if we've got eternity to waste - otherwise how would we get through the next five minutes?

AGLAYA: That's exactly the opposite of the moral the Prince was hinting at. Isn't it, Prince?

(Stares at him.)

Well - do you live every moment as if it were your last?

MYSHKIN (after a pause): Sometimes I think I can.

AGLAYA: And are you thinking so now?

MYSHKIN: Yes.

AGLAYA: And are we very beautiful to you? Like those sunbeams?

(MYSHKIN looks at her intently, nods, looks down in confusion.

Laughs.)

You see – he's practising what he was preaching.

ADELAIDA: Have you seen lots of beautiful girls, Prince?

AGLAYA: Of course he has. He makes them beautiful by looking at them as if they were the last sight he was going to see.

MRS YEPANCHIN: Aglaya!

ADELAIDA: But any specially beautiful?

MYSHKIN: Well, there was a girl in the village where my clinic was. In Switzerland.

ALEXANDRIA: And were you in love with her?

MYSHKIN (nods slowly): I think I loved her.

ADELAIDA: Well, what was she like?

ALEXANDRIA: Was she engaged to someone else? What happened?

MYSHKIN: She was dying of tuberculosis.

ADELAIDA: How dreadful.

MYSHKIN: And all the people in the village – you see, she had a child, an illegitimate child, and they hated her for it, and they threw stones at her. But – she was so – always gentle and frightened – she was beautiful.

ALEXANDRIA: And you loved her?

AGLAYA: Of course he did – although he'd probably have loved her even more if she'd been the mother of illegitimate twins and had a club foot as well.

MRS YEPANCHIN (shocked): Aglaya!

AGLAYA: But, mother, it's not fair – he's showing off, that's all.

MRS YEPANCHIN: No he's not –

(Stares at AGLAYA.)

– and what's more, you know it.

ADELAIDA: Have you seen any other beautiful women, Prince?

ALEXANDRIA: Yes, tell us. Here, in St Petersburg, have you?

MRS YEPANCHIN: Now, Prince, don't you dare give them the answer they're waiting for.

MYSHKIN: Well, yes, yes, I've seen one very beautiful woman.

ADELAIDA: Who? Here? In St Petersburg?

ALEXANDRIA: Where? Who is she? Do you know her name?

MYSHKIN: Well, of course - I've only seen her picture - when General Yepanchin and Mr Ivolgin were going to test my handwriting - ?

MRS YEPANCHIN: Test your handwriting?

MYSHKIN: Yes, there was a little misunderstanding - well -

MRS YEPANCHIN: But why did they test your handwriting?

MYSHKIN: Oh no, they didn't, because then I saw the picture - but they wanted to see if my handwriting was good enough so that I could replace Mr Ivolgin as the General's secretary - and then I saw the picture -

MRS YEPANCHIN: Whose pic -

(Stops, as if realizing.)

MYSHKIN: Um, Nastasya Filippovna's -

(There is a ghastly silence. As lights go down on the dining-room.)

FERDYSCHENKO: Well done, well done, Prince. Yes, I think you made an impression there, all right.

(He laughs, as lights rise on the living-room where GANYA is still sitting at the desk.)

Scene Six

The Bar

Lights up.

There is shouting, cheering etc. , as ROGOZHIN strides into the bar, followed by KELLER and LEBEDEV escorting in the MONEY-LENDER and the ROGUES pushing in behind them.

MONEY-LENDER: There. You see? All for Mr Rogozhin.

(He puts his case on the floor.

ROGUES, held back by KELLER, gather round it. He opens the case. There is a gasp.)

FERDYSCHENKO (who has been watching): Sir, sir, excuse me, sir, I understand you're anxious to know the name of the lucky bridegroom?

ROGOZHIN: What? What? Well, man. Come on!

(Thumps table.

FERDYSCHENKO coughs.

ROGOZHIN takes money out of the case.)

FERDYSCHENKO: Thank you, sir.

(Comes over, whispers into ROGOZHIN's ear, as.)

MONEY-LENDER: Five roubles!

(As it is given to FERDYSCHENKO.)

Mark it down!

ROGOZHIN: What! that little swine! I know him! I know that little swine!

FERDYSCHENKO: And I can also tell you...

ROGUES: Sssshh!

FERDYSCHENKO: Where you can find him.

ROGOZHIN: Count! Count!

(Banging on the table.)

What have you got there?

MONEY-LENDER: Fifty thousand roubles...

ROGOZHIN: How much? Only fifty thousand.

(Leans over, grabs MONEY-LENDER.)

Where's the rest of it?

MONEY-LENDER: But, sir, this gentleman said fifty thousand...

(Indicates LEBEDEV.)

LEBEDEV: I'm sure Nastasya Filippovna can be had for even less – speaking with your financial interests at heart...

ROGOZHIN (knocks LEBEDEV side-ways, bellows): I said one hundred thousand for my Princess! One hundred thousand!

MONEY-LENDER: But, sir, I would have to go to my office...

ROGOZHIN (propelling MONEY-LENDER towards the door):

One hundred thousand –

(Pushes him out, cries off.)

ROGUES: One hundred thousand, one hundred thousand, kill,
kill, etc.

(Exeunt.)

FERDYSCHENKO: You see? A sweet simple creature who
believes that human beings can be bought.

(Pause.)

Hey! I'm for sale.

Scene Seven

The YEPANCHIN Living-room.

Lights up.

AGLAYA meanwhile has come into the living-room, where
GANYA is writing. Stands, watching him.

AGLAYA: Mr Ivolgin?

GANYA (becomes aware of AGLAYA, turns, gets up, then holding
the note, walks towards her pleadingly): Aglaya! I was just
writing to you –

AGLAYA (ignores the note): We shall be needing this room, Mr
Ivolgin. We want to test your replacement.

(As GANYA tries to thrust his note on her again.)

So you see –

(Ignoring it again.)

– we're no longer interested in your handwriting.

(GANYA follows her, as.)

GANYA: Aglaya – don't – excuse me.

(ADELAIDA, ALEXANDRIA, MRS YEPANCHIN, MYSHKIN
enter. They stop, as they see GANYA and AGLAYA.

GANYA picks up the picture and note, walks out of the room.)

ADELAIDA: But what shall we make him write?

ALEXANDRIA: Something funny. Come on, Prince -

> (Leads him to the table. MRS YEPANCHIN and ADELAIDA, looking at AGLAYA, follow.)

AGLAYA: Just a minute, I want to see the portrait, please.

> (They look at her.)

> Well, is no one going to get it? Will you get it please, Prince, from Ganya?

> (MYSHKIN looks from one to the other.)

MRS YEPANCHIN: No, I forbid this. I don't want to have any- thing to do with what those - those childish -

> (Stops.)

> Get it, Prince.

> (As MYSHKIN goes off.)

> I'm very weak.

> (There is a silence, they all look away from each other. MYSHKIN half-steps back into the room, the picture under his arm, then the sound of GANYA's voice. He steps out again, another pause, reappears. Stands with the picture.

> Looks at AGLAYA then walks over. MYSHKIN gives the picture to MRS YEPANCHIN.)

> Thank you, Prince.

> (GANYA appears quietly at the door.

> AGLAYA has turned her back.)

ALEXANDRIA: But she's beautiful!

> (MYSHKIN goes over to AGLAYA, attempts to hand her the note secretly, drops it, picks it up, attempts to give it to her again. MRS YEPANCHIN, GANYA, ADELAIDA and ALEXANDRIA all see this performance.)

AGLAYA: What's this?

MYSHKIN: From Ganya...

> (Aloud. Opens the note, places it on the small table.)

MRS YEPANCHIN (suddenly seeing GANYA): Yes, Mr Ivolgin?

GANYA: I - I - I - the General suggested the Prince take a room with my family if he has nowhere to stay.

(Glances at AGLAYA.)

MYSHKIN: That is very kind of you. Thank you.

(GANYA nods, makes as if to withdraw.)

MRS YEPANCHIN: Yes, I see. Well, give my regards to your unfortunate mother. Come along, Prince, show us your handwriting.

(MYSHKIN goes over to the desk, followed by MRS YEPANCHIN, ADELAIDA, ALEXANDRIA.

AGLAYA walks over to the picture, picks it up, looks at it. GANYA comes over to her.

MYSHKIN is ready, pen dipped in ink, paper before him etc.)

MRS YEPANCHIN: Now, Prince, write something very clever.

AGLAYA: Please write: 'I do not bargain with mercenary cowards. '

(MYSHKIN looks at her, startled.

Coming to the desk.)

I do not bargain with mercenary cowards.

(MYSHKIN writes. Blots the page.

Takes the page.)

Yes, he will make an admirable replacement, won't he?

(To GANYA as she hands him the page, and walks on out of the room.)

MRS YEPANCHIN: Aglaya, don't be so rude.

ADELAIDA: No, no! Mother, don't, she's upset, she's crying.

ALEXANDRIA: Don't worry, Prince, it'll be alright.

MRS YEPANCHIN: I'm sorry, Prince, it's nothing, at least, anyway, it's not your fault. Please forgive us. You're a dear good boy and I like you very, very much.

ALEXANDRIA: Come along, Mother.

(MRS YEPANCHIN, ADELAIDA and ALEXANDRIA go out.

GANYA stares at MYSHKIN, getting up from his desk.

MYSHKIN stands by himself, staring around the empty room. Then sees his bundle, goes to pick it up.)

GANYA (stares at him): You – you – clumsy... or did you let everyone see it on purpose? To work your way into the family! Is that it? Is it money you're after, or more medical treatment, you – you idiot!

MYSHKIN (looks at him): You may not address me like that.

GANYA: Forgive me, Prince.

(Looks at him.)

I – I didn't mean it. I can see you don't mean any harm. Come, let's be friends.

MYSHKIN (smiles): I should like to be your friend.

GANYA: You see – I begged her to give me a sign, that's all. Just a sign.

MYSHKIN: A sign?

GANYA: That she'd marry me if I gave up – Nastasya Filippovna. If I refused to go through with it.

MYSHKIN: Marry you – you mean Miss Aglaya? You're – are you in love with Miss Aglaya?

GANYA: Do you think I haven't the right? because I'm poor?

MYSHKIN: No – no – of course you have the right.

GANYA: Yes, but she wants me to give up Nastasya Filippovna without telling me whether she'll marry me or not. Then if she didn't, what would I have? What? But it doesn't matter. It's too late. My engagement will be announced this evening.

(Laughs.)

The happiest moment –

MYSHKIN: Then you don't love Nastasya Filippovna – not at all?

GANYA: Love her? Totsky's woman?

(Laughs.)

MYSHKIN: But she's not Totsky's woman. He took her when she was just a child. He made her a prisoner for his bed – it's not her fault – she had no choice.

GANYA: But she's still his whore. I loathe her, Prince!

MYSHKIN: Then give her up – give her up – for pity's sake!

GANYA: But don't you see, Prince? I have no choice. A poor

man never does. Not pity. I can't afford it. I've got to have money!

(Stares at MYSHKIN as lights go down on them and up on FERDYSCHENKO.)

Scene Eight

NASTASYA's Party

CHEREVSKY: Yes. Yes. Yes. Thirty thousand.

PTITSYN: Thirty thousand!

CHEREVSKY: Thirty thousand roubles. And why not? Lots of loving guardians have given their little wards larger dowries.

PTITSYN (laughs): Poor old Totsky! That'll teach him to take orphaned waifs under his roof.

GONCHAREV: And think what she's already cost him in food and clothing.

(Laughter.)

CHEREVSKY: Oh, but she's worked for it.

(Laughter.)

What's Totsky's phrase? 'Brightened his home. ' She's 'brightened his home', you know. That takes work.

(Laughter.)

PTITSYN: But still thirty thousand. He must be desperate.

GONCHAREV: And so's Ganya Ivolgin. For the thirty thousand.

(Laughter as DARIA, KRETCHLIFF, YECHARIN drift on stage laughing, holding drinks.)

CHEREVSKY: Ah, Daria.

(Goes over, gives her a kiss.)

How is she? What's she going to do tonight? Submit with maidenly modesty or give us a scene to remember?

PTITSYN: With that famous paper-knife, eh? Have another go at him with it?

(Laughter.)

DARIA: Now you stop it, all of you! This is a very solemn occasion.

CHEREVSKY: Of course it is! By the way, where's the lucky bridegroom? Or is he being bashful?

(More laughter which stops as -)

TOTSKY (enters through the door): Good evening. 'Evening, Ptitsyn, nice to see you.

(To DARIA.)

She's not here yet, then? Anything wrong?

DARIA: Don't worry. It's going to be alright. She's going to be alright!

TOTSKY: I hope so. But frankly, I won't be happy until the evening's safely over.

YEPANCHIN (enters): Good evening - Hello, Nastasya's not with us? And where's Ganya?

DARIA: Really, YOU men! Anyone would think it was your engagement that was going to be announced.

(Enter CRIPPLES.)

YEPANCHIN: Who on earth... ?

TOTSKY: Oh, just charity cases left over from her last religious phase.

CHEREVSKY: Good heavens!

(Laughs.)

I must say, Nastasya's got an extraordinary gift for people - or a gift for extraordinary people. And situations. Do you remember the night at the Opera House when that demented ... Rogozhin... was prowling up and down the aisle beneath her box groaning 'Nastasya, Nastasya, my Princess my Queen. '

(The door opens. NASTASYA appears, magnificently but simply dressed, with the necklace at her throat.)

NASTASYA: Good evening.

(Laughs, shouts of 'Good evening, Nastasya'.)

I'm sorry I'm late, my darlings, I just wanted to give you time to lay your bets. What odds are you giving, Kretchliff?

TOTSKY (goes to her): My dear – my dear, you look simply ravishing. It's worth the wait.

(Takes her hand to kiss it.)

NASTASYA: Thank you, my dear.

(Amidst laughter.)

Ah, Daria, and Kretchliff. Ah, and the General, how nice to see you.

(Gives him her hand.)

YEPANCHIN (kissing it): And may I say, Nastasya Filippovna, how lovely, how very lovely... very very lovely...

NASTASYA: Thank you, General. When you say it, I believe it. The General's a great connoisseur of what ladies should wear, aren't you, General?

(Laughs.)

But are we all here? Ganya. Here's my Ganya.

(GANYA enters the room through the door, takes her hand, kisses it.)

NASTASYA: I hope you liked your present.

(Kisses him, laughs, claps.)

It's absurdly flattering.

(To TOTSKY.)

Don't you think so, guardian? Doesn't it make you quite proud of me.

TOTSKY: I'm quite proud enough as it is.

(Takes his hand, puts his other hand through GANYA's arm.)

Very proud indeed. Ladies and gentlemen – my friends, especially those of you who remember Nastasya when she first brightened my home by coming into it, you must all have guessed by now why this is to be one of the happiest evenings of my life.

(Laughter, bravos, claps.)

My Nastasya and this young man beside me –

NASTASYA: Oh good heavens, guardian, guardian, just a minute. I see some very special friends I must speak to first.

(Goes to the lame and blind.)

My dears, are you alright there? Are you comfortable? Have you enough to eat?

BLIND MAN: Oh yes, thank you, Nastasya, and so honoured.

NASTASYA: Vera, how lovely the shawl is you made for me. I was so touched.

CRIPPLED LADY: You look beautiful, Nastasya Filippovan. And your necklace –

CRIPPLED MAN: Is nearly as beautiful as the throat it adorns.

NASTASYA (laughs): Thank you. Each one of you. I should have been so unhappy if you hadn't been able to come tonight.

BLIND MAN: Bless you, Nastasya Filippovna, bless you.

NASTASYA: But the rest of you all look so bored. Are you? But you mustn't be. Shall we play a game? Would you like that? Yes, let's play a game. Ferdyschenko knows a marvellous new one. You'll love it. I know you will.

GUESTS (laughing to each other): Game! What's she up to? What game?

TOTSKY: My dear, don't you think –

NASTASYA: Where's my Ferdyschenko? Ferdyschenko! Show yourself!

FERDYSCHENKO (comes forward): Here, dear girl, here!

(Comes, stands beside NASTASYA.)

PTITSYN: How the devil did you get in here.

FERDYSCHENKO: Oh, I have the entreé. I have the entreé.

NASTASYA: Explain it to them, Ferdyschenko. You know the one.

(Whispers to him.)

TOTSKY (laughing with false indulgence): My dear, may I just make my little announcement –

NASTASYA: No, I want to play it now. Now. It's terribly simple. You must all join in – everybody in the room – all you have to do is to describe the most shameful thing you've ever done, and the winner, well, the winner is the one who tells the most shocking story about himself. Isn't that right,

Ferdyschenko, that's all they have to do, isn't it, be appalling.

FERDYSCHENKO: It's very fashionable in the salons of Paris and some of our lower bars.

(Laughs.)

Shall I begin? To set the tone?

TOTSKY: Frankly, my dear, it doesn't sound a very enjoyable game, and we do have something more important on our minds.

FERDYSCHENKO: The champagne, he means.

NASTASYA: Yes, yes, you begin –

(Clapping her hands.)

– and then I shall choose the person who comes next. I give you, Ferdyschenko.

FERDYSCHENKO (laughter): I shall be brief. My most shameful act.

(Laughter.)

No, one of my more shameful acts.

(More laughter.)

Two years ago, when I was staying with a friend – no, I must be truthful – that's the only rule, after all – when I was staying with a chance acquaintance on whom I'd imposed myself –

(Laughter.)

– one evening, while the ten-year-old daugher of the household was charming the more susceptible with a song at the piano and I was on my way to the kitchens for a drink –

(Laughter.)

– I happened to come across my hostess's handbag unattended on her desk. I slipped my hand in it, it came out with three roubles closely attached. Sweat, you see. I always sweat when I steal.

(Titters.)

And when this trifling sum was missed by the lady of the house –

(Very few titters, uncertain.)

- I managed to get one of her maids - a sensitive, tongue-tied creature, accused of it. I assisted at her interrogation and sent her packing.

(There is an appalled silence.)

TOTSKY: My God!

YEPANCHIN: I've never heard anything -

NASTASYA (laughs, begins to clap): I think that's a very promising beginning.

FERDYSCHENKO: Thank you, thank you, what's the prize?

NASTASYA: Not yet, darling, there are some passionate competitors in the room. I think my own Ganya can beat you. Ganya, darling, be more appalling than Ferdyschenko.

GANYA: Thank you, Nastasya Filippovna, I'd rather not.

NASTASYA: Oh, but Ganya, please, sweet. Afterwards we shall have my guardian, won't we, guardian, and then the General, and then Ptitsyn can tell us his favourite farmyard story - the one about yourself you've never told before, and Admiral, why you've stopped going to sea, you used to love the foreign ports, and Kretchliff, my dear Ygor, what you did yesterday, or the day before, if it comes to that, whichever is the more disgusting... but you must go first, darling, please.

TOTSKY: The fact is, my dear, this is a very critical moment in Ganya's...

NASTASYA: Ganya, tell your story. Don't be afraid of boring us.

(Sharply.)

Tell it!

(There is a pause, NASTASYA looking at GANYA, when.)

MAID (opening the door): Madame, the Prince Leo Nikolaievich Myshkin.

(MYSHKIN appears at the door, still dressed as before. Stands hesitantly on the threshold. Company turns, some laughter.)

TOTSKY (to YEPANCHIN): Good God, it's the idiot. What the

Hell...?

MYSHKIN (stares at NASTASYA): Nastasya Filippovna. Nastasya Filippovna. Forgive me, please. Forgive me.

(Comes forward.)

I - I followed Ganya and then I got lost.

(Ripples of laughter.)

Some people kindly showed me - I had to come. I had to see you. I'm sorry, I'm...

NASTASYA: But do you know me? Have we met?

MYSHKIN: No. No. But I've seen your picture and - and - and I've been thinking about you. I've been thinking about you. All day.

NASTASYA: Thinking about me?

GANYA: What the hell do you mean following me everywhere. Get out of here - you weren't invited.

NASTASYA: Leave him alone. He's invited now. Katia, Champagne for the Prince.

MYSHKIN: No, Nastasya! You see, I must tell you...I must...

NASTASYA: What? What must you tell me?

(MYSHKIN laughs. After a moment, general laughter.)

NASTASYA: I see I amuse you.

MYSHKIN: I'm - I'm...please, sometimes I - my face laughs when I'm not laughing at all. Things come out the opposite of what I'm feeling. It's an... affliction.

NASTASYA: Do you mean that really you're crying?

(Laughter.)

YEPANCHIN: The Prince has just returned from a Swiss Clinic. He's not well.

FERDYSCHENKO: I hear this kind of wooing's very fashionable in Switzerland.

(More laughter.)

MYSHKIN: I know how much you've had to suffer. I know you're suffering...ever since I heard of you...and what you're suffering now – at this minute... it must be terrible for you, terrible, I know that. I know you.

NASTASYA (amidst laughter): Suffering? My suffering?

MYSHKIN: Isn't it true? isn't it true, Nastasya? You don't belong here, you're not like this.

NASTASYA: No, Prince, I'm not like this, I'm worse – far worse. My friends, a perfect judge has come for our game. All the way from a Swiss Clinic – the crying judge with the laughing face. Prince, you will be our judge.

MYSHKIN: Judge... judge... what should I judge?

NASTASYA: Why, my Ganya's story. He's too shy to tell us himself, but I'm sure you know it, everybody knows it, tell us how you judge a man who is prepared for a trifling consideration to take on Totsky's woman, the whore of St Petersburg!

(Exclamations, gasps and laughs from the guests as.)

MYSHKIN: Don't – don't speak like that! You're not – you're not –

NASTASYA: Answer me! Answer me! I've made you my judge!

MYSHKIN: But what – what can I – what do you want?

NASTASYA: Why, your decision as to whether I'm to marry him or not. That's what they've all come to hear.

MYSHKIN (his mouth working, looks at GANYA, looks back at NASTASYA): I came – I came – to tell you – to beg you – not to marry – not to marry Ganya.

NASTASYA: You see, a real Prince. Thank you. Thank you, Prince.

TOTSKY: But really – this is too preposterous.

GANYA (simultaneously): And thank you for the extraordinary delicacy with which you've let this – I realise a poor man isn't entitled to – to anything.

NASTASYA (laughs): Nothing. Nothing. Not even a dowry, little secretary, it's writing other people's letter for life, for you –

TOTSKY: This is madness!

NASTASYA: Oh, oh, and this man, Prince, you mustn't forget to judge him. The man who looked after me when I was an orphan, who took me into his own house, and clothed me, and fed me, as he's so fond of telling people, and what else did you do, guardian? That people are so fond of telling each other about? And how do you judge him, Prince, do you judge him worthy of dear little Adelaida, the virgin daughter of his best friend?

MYSHKIN: I - I - Mr Totsky is a - a -

NASTASYA: You see, he can't say it. But what about the General. A man who would have my Mr Totsky for his son-in-law? How do you judge him?

MYSHKIN: I think - I think - General Yepanchin is a kind man.

NASTASYA: Yes, yes, -

(Laughing.)

- they're all kind men. You see, the Prince has judged you and now I shall set you free. You, guardian, are free to marry any good girl you want, without even the expense of a dowry for me. And you, General, - here -

(Undoing the necklace from her neck.)

- are free to give this to some other lady, two conquests with one gift! And you, darling, are free -

(To GANYA.)

- no, you will never be free, you poor little thing. But I am, yes, free at last - free from you, and you, and you, free never to spend one single rouble of yours again, or spend one more day in this apartment, free to walk out of the door and into the street, free to earn my living as a washer-woman, yes, a washer-woman. And if I can't do that, if you've spoiled me for that, why then I'll be a licensed prostitute rather than owe anything more to you, or you, or you!

(MYSHKIN is staring at her, eyes alight.

Simultaneously there is a crashing noise outside, chaos. The MAID throws the door open, screaming as:

ROGOZHIN with LEBEDEV, KELLER and the gang of ROGUES come in.)

KRETCHLIF: Anarchists! Anarchists!

CHEREVSKY: My God, whatever next!

(Other guests move back, with exclamations of fear as.)

ROGOZHIN: Where is she? Where is she?

(Turns, sees NASTASYA. He walks towards her reverently, carrying a paper bundle.)

For you, my Princess - my Queen - for you.

LEBEDEV: One hundred thousand roubles.

(Guests exclaim 'Good God!' 'One hundred thousand what?' etc.)

GANYA (laughs contemptuously): Rogozhin! How appropriate!

ROGOZHIN (turns, looks at him): Why it's the little swine. I've been hearing all about you, little swine! I've got something for you.

(Takes out a knife.

Guests' screams of 'My God!' etc.)

ROGOZHIN and ROGUES: Kill him, kill him, kill him!

ROGOZHIN (steps towards GANYA, roars with laughter, puts the knife away, draws out a note from his pocket): No, you're not worth that. This is what you're worth! Here, take it! It's yours.

(Turns to NASTASYA, holds out the bundle again.)

I've come back to you, Nastasya Filippovna. As you knew I would. I've come back to you.

LEBEDEV: With one hundred thousand roubles!

ROGOZHIN: Do you come with me then? Eh? Eh?

LEBEDEV: For a hundred thousand roubles!

NASTASYA (laughs): See how my value rises - see - from thirty thousand roubles to a hundred thousand.

ROGOZHIN: And more! More!

LEBEDEV: Much more! A million and a half!

NASTASYA: So you're all agreed, then? I sell myself to the highest bidder, one hundred thousand roubles and a promise of a million and a half, to Mr Parfyon Rogozhin! Is that what you agree, is it, is it?

GUESTS: A million and a half!

(Laughter.)

That's a hell of a price, etc., etc.

ROGOZHIN: Well! Well!

(Drunk with triumph.)

Is that it then? Have I done it then? Have I? Have I?

(ROGUES roaring hurrahs, the guests now laughing, the charity cases crying out. DARIA comes to NASTASYA, embraces her.)

FERDYSCHENKO: Going! Going! Going!

MYSHKIN (who has been blocked off by the ROGUES, suddenly cries out, though not seen): Nastasya – Nastasya –

NASTASYA: What?

MYSHKIN: Excuse me, forgive me, I'm very sorry.

(As he stumbles between the guests, apologizing.)

NASTASYA: But of course, my judge. I've forgotten my judge. I can't conclude the deal without consulting him.

ROGOZHIN: What?

(Bewildered, sees MYSHKIN, peers at him, throws out his arms with a cry.)

Why, it's – it's my little Prince!

(Embraces MYSHKIN.)

My Prince with the Holy Face – See, see what I told you? I've done it, I've done it. Eh?

NASTASYA: Well, Prince – does he buy me then?

(ROGOZHIN laughs, ROGUES laugh.)

You see, I'm waiting for your word.

MYSHKIN: You – no, you must not go with him. You must not.

ROGOZHIN (laughing again, incredulous): Why, little Prince...

NASTASYA: Ahh! And why must I not?

MYSHKIN: Because it's not what you want. Because you want to be free. Because – because – he – it would make him so unhappy too.

(Looking at ROGOZHIN.)

Because –

FERDYSCHENKO: Because you want to marry her yourself.

(Suddenly pushing through.

Shouts of laughter.)

MYSHKIN (nods, smiling): Yes. Yes, I want to marry you, Nastasya Filippovna.

(ROGOZHIN, ROGUES, GUESTS all laughing.)

NASTASYA: You? Marry me?

MYSHKIN: Marry you.

NASTASYA: But you see, they're laughing at you for wanting to marry me.

(Very gently.)

They're all laughing at you.

ROGOZHIN (goes to MYSHKIN, nuzzles him affectionately): He's an idiot, Princess. A holy idiot.

(Stands with his arm around him.)

Don't worry, Prince. We'll look after you.

NASTASYA: Are you an idiot, Prince? Is that why they laugh?

MYSHKIN: Perhaps – perhaps – I don't know – But I want to marry a remarkable woman, a good woman.

(Looking around.)

A woman who has been made to suffer. Is that the desire of an idiot? Nastasya Filippovna, I respect you above – above – I love you. I am ready to die for you.

FERDYSCHENKO: That's the desire of an idiot.

(Renewed laughter.)

ROGOZHIN: Shut up, shut up – he's a good man, a holy man. And he knows a woman when he sees one. I honour him!

NASTASYA: Should I marry him, then?

ROGOZHIN: What? Princess –

(Laughing.)

NASTASYA: As my judge has made an offer himself, someone else will have to judge for him. Guardian – what should I do? Should I marry the Prince?

TOTSKY: Certainly, my dear. If it suits your mood to marry a sick pauper.

MYSHKIN (amidst laughter): No – no – I'm not – at least, you see, I think I'm – I may be very rich.

FERDYSCHENKO: The riches stored in Heaven aren't negotiable here.

MYSHKIN: No – look – here, I've got this letter – I have it, I don't completely understand it but –

ROGOZHIN: Princess – come with me now. Come now. A million and a half. Of this. As much as we'll need –

LEBEDEV: And more! And more!

(YEPANCHIN takes the letter, reads it out.)

YEPANCHIN: But, my dear, not as much as Prince Myshkin can offer you. He stands to inherit – from the estate of his late guardian, Leo David Pavlischev, a fortune estimated at three and a half million roubles. Three and a half million roubles my dear.

(There is a stunned silence.)

LEBEDEV: And such Christ loveth! And such Christ loveth!

YEPANCHIN: My dear fellow, congratulations, Mrs Yepanchin will be delighted –

TOTSKY: My friends. We have one of the richest men in Russia with us tonight.

(This through mutterings, exclamations, etc., from guests.)

NASTASYA: Well, Rogozhin – you've been outbid. I'm to be the Prince's Princess.

ROGOZHIN (is staring at MYSHKIN, transfixed): No, no, no! No!

(Laughter.)

Prince, please, I – please don't take her from me. Prince. Please let me have her. Please!

(More laughter from the guests.)

NASTASYA: Well, Prince, are you going to let him have me? Now that he's given up buying for begging?

MYSHKIN: He loves you very much, Nastasya.

ROGOZHIN (sinks to his knees, amidst new laughter): Princess, please.

(Holds the money out to her, then turns on his knees, drops the money at MYSHKIN's feet.)

Please - Prince - Please.

KELLER (gently lifts him up): On your feet, sir. This isn't worthy of a man of honour, sir.

(Shouts.)

Parfyon Rogozhin is a man of great passion!

MYSHKIN: I'm sorry - I'm very sorry, Parfyon. But you see, no good would come of it. No good for either of you. Please forgive me for the pain you're feeling now. Please forgive me.

NASTASYA: And could you forgive me for all that has happened here this evening? Could you ever forget what I have been and that everybody in this room, will laugh whenever my name is mentioned.

MYSHKIN: I shall always remember, Nastasya. I shall remember this night all our lives as the night when you honoured me, from your goodness. And as for people laughing - well, I shan't mind. I shall be proud.

NASTASYA: Well, my friends, what shall I do? Shall I marry the Prince, my friends. Shall I? Shall I? Shall I?

(Takes MYSHKIN's hand.)

No one has ever spoken to me as you have. And I shall remember this evening all my life, for what you have said to me. No one has ever spoken of honour, love, respect. Thank you, Prince.

(Turns.)

Well, Rogozhin, I accept your offer. Shall we be on our way.

ROGOZHIN (in stunned silence, then exclamations): Wha - wha - wha! What! What!

MYSHKIN (makes a move towards NASTASYA): Nastasya, don't don't, don't!

ROGOZHIN: Don't touch - don't touch - you heard her - I've

won! She's mine!

MYSHKIN: Nastasya, you mustn't –

ROGOZHIN: Shut up, shut up, shut up, idiot!

NASTASYA: How dare you! You do not speak to the Prince like that!

(To ROGOZHIN, who cowers back.)

Goodbye, Prince. You see, I belong with him. That's where I belong.

GANYA: Yes, you do. And may I wish you the happiness you deserve with him.

GONCHAREV: But that's the bridegroom.

NASTASYA (looks at GANYA, then snatches the parcel of money from the floor): And you – here is the happiness you crave. Would you like it? Would you? Here!

(GANYA stares at her, and at the money.)

A hundred thousand! More than you ever dreamed of! Here! Take it!

GUESTS: What? She's giving it to him. She must be mad.

NASTASYA: Well.

(She begins to walk towards the fire.)

Come – reach for it – touch it and you shall have it – come – come –

(GANYA follows her like an automaton.)

There!

(Shakes it in front of him, and as his arm comes up, throws the money into the fire.

ROGOZHIN roars with laughter, as.)

GUESTS: No, no, it'll burn. She must be made. Should we tie her up!

TOTSKY (to himself): My God, what a woman, what a woman!

NASTASYA: Quick, little clerk, get it, get it!

BLIND MAN (on his feet, turning his head about wildly): What's she done, what's she done? I smell – is it the money? Is it?

LEBEDEV: I'll do it, madame Princess, I'll get it out with my teeth!

FERDYSCHENKO: Me, let me get it for you, ten per cent, that's all I ask.

LEBEDEV (to GANYA): Five - five per cent!

(FERDYSCHENKO suddenly springs forward.)

ROGOZHIN: Keller!

(KELLER grabs FERDYSCHENKO, pulls him back from the fire.

LEBEDEV drops to his knees, scrambles towards the fire, KELLER restrains him.

There is a sudden silence, as:

GANYA staring down at the grate, puts out his arm, then lets out a cry, crashes backwards, in a faint.)

NASTASYA: Well, so his vanity is greater than his greed.

(Grabs the tongs, pulls the bundle out of the fire, drops it in the grate.)

Give it to him.

ROGOZHIN: I told you she was mine. My Queen.

NASTASYA (gives her arm to ROGOZHIN): And the rest of you take what you like. A present from the whore.

(ROGOZHIN, yelling in triumph, followed by shouting ROGUES and KELLER, sweeps her out of the room. As she goes.)

MYSHKIN: No - no - Nastasya -

(MYSHKIN makes to run after them, is held back.

LEBEDEV looking back after the money, runs out of the room.

FERDYSCHENKO is beating at the flames at the edge of the money.

GANYA has been assisted to his feet.

MYSHKIN is standing, watching him, awkwardly.

LEBEDEV brings the money to GANYA, as:

FERDYSCHENKO is swiping a bottle of champagne, whilst

other guests loot NASTASYA's apartment.

GANYA and MYSHKIN stand embracing, as LEBEDEV is watching them and then leaves.)

GANYA: Prince - help me - for God's sake! Help me.

FERDYSCHENKO (dusting himself down, clutching a champagne bottle, staggering slightly): What an evening, what an evening! Magnificent gestures, moral heroics, tantrums! Sudden fortunes, fainting fits, sing-songs, singeing hair, champagne - champagne, champagne!

(Drinks some.)

Aaaah - aaaah - the party's over, the party's ended - but lives, lives don't stop when the champagne's run out. At least, passionate lives don't. Passionate lives go passionately on! Ladies and gentlemen, I give you St Petersburg's most notorious, most flamboyant pair of sinners with a month of passion behind them.

Scene Nine

ROGOZHIN's Room

Lights go up on ROGOZHIN's room, NASTASYA in a wrap, playing cards.

ROGOZHIN: What are you looking at?

NASTASYA: I'm looking at you. I'm thinking about the Prince and I'm looking at you.

ROGOZHIN: He's a holy idiot.

NASTASYA: Is he?

ROGOZHIN (after they play for a while): You win.

(Smiling anxiously.)

NASTASYA: I always win. Is that because you let me?

ROGOZHIN: What? Let you?

(Laughs.)

It's because I'm stupid.

(After they play a while.)

NASTASYA: One hundred thousand roubles.

(Laughs.)

Is this how I'm to earn it to the end of our lives?

ROGOZHIN: See, now I'm winning. But you wanted to play. You said you did.

NASTASYA: And what would <u>you</u> like to do, Parfyon?

ROGOZHIN I - I

(Staring at her.)

- love you, Nastasya.

NASTASYA (looks at him, laughs, plays. After a moment): Did you love me when Lebedev told you I'd been to bed with Captain -

ROGOZHIN: Don't!

NASTASYA (going on playing): Or did you realise then what you'd bought for your hundred thousand roubles? You bought a whore, Parfyon. You must expect me to behave whorishly. I can't play cards with you every evening. Play! Or shall I go out. Do you think the Prince would honour me now, Parfyon, if he knew how many men I've deceived you with?

(Laughs.)

Sometimes I go with men to forget that there is someone who honours me. <u>And sometimes I go with them to forget you.</u>

ROGOZHIN (hitting her, knocking her to the ground): Please!

NASTASYA (crouches on the floor): What's the matter, Parfyon? Don't you like your bargain? Aren't I cheap enough -

ROGOZHIN (hits her again and again and again, sinking to his knees): Don't - please - please - don't -

(They both remain on the floor, then NASTASYA, climbs to her feet, looks down at him.)

Forgive me!

NASTASYA: Look at him, grovelling on his knees to his whore, full of murder for his whore!

ROGOZHIN: Forgive me!

NASTASYA: Don't beg, Parfyon.

(Bends over him contemptuously.)

Kill me! Kill me now!

(Offers him her throat, kicks him.)

Now! Now! You'll do it in the end, do it now!

ROGOZHIN (shaking his head, stumbles to her on his knees, raises the hem of her wrap to his lips): Forgive me, Nastasya!

NASTASYA: Kill me!

(Screams, looking down at him, then as he doesn't move, runs out of the room.

NASTASYA stands in the room.)

FERDYSCHENKO: Well, she can't play cards with him every night. But what could it be that's lured her out in the deshabille?

(Laughs.)

Oh, you can't corrupt a whore with money or sex. But you can do it with three words - three words and an idiot smile. Honour! Respect! Love! God has always had an ugly way of loosening the tongues of idiots, and making them the salvation of sinners. I know the type. I know the type.

Scene Ten

MYSHKIN's Room

Lights up on MYSHKIN and NASTASYA.

NASTASYA (walking up and down in a fervour): And do you still believe it? In spite of everything I've told you?

MYSHKIN: Yes, I do believe it. I know it.

NASTASYA (standing with her back to him): Then tell me again, Prince. Please.

MYSHKIN: Nastasya, all the things that you have done that you hate yourself for, all your pain, all your anger. That is because you're good. What is goodness but wanting to be good? You have had to fight so hard. You are good, Nastasya. You are a good woman.

NASTASYA (claps her hands enthusiastically): I don't know if I
am good, but when you say it, I believe it too. I believe I
can be. It's as if I'd waited all my life for someone - for
you - to say the words. You see, you've made me so - so
happy, Leo Nikolaievich -

(Turns, takes his hand.)

How can I make you happy too?

MYSHKIN: By - letting me love you. By - by marrying me,
Nastasya.

NASTASYA: Do you promise me that is what you really want?

MYSHKIN: Yes. Yes. And then perhaps Parfyon would be free
again and could live his life again. And you - you could find
peace, Nastasya. I think I might bring you peace.

NASTASYA: But I. What would I bring you? Look at me - tell
me what could I bring you?

MYSHKIN: I would love you all my life.

(NASTASYA after a pause, raises his hand to her lips,
kisses it sadly. Then turns away.)

Nastasya? What's the matter?

NASTASYA: It's too late, it's too late.

(Sobbing.)

I'm not - I'm not.

MYSHKIN: Don't, Nastasya, don't. Don't.

NASTASYA (embraces him passionately, sobbing): I love you,
Prince. I love you, I love you.

(MYSHKIN stands awkwardly in her embrace.

NASTASYA steps away, looks at him, then puts her hands
to her face.

MYSHKIN goes to her, takes her hands away from her face,
then holding her hands, goes down on his knees.)

MYSHKIN: I love you too, Nastasya. If I've offended you please
forgive me.

NASTASYA: I mustn't, I mustn't - I am not good, I am not good.
Oh - oh - oh - God!

(Wails out, turns, runs out of the room.)

MYSHKIN: Nastasya, Nastasya, forgive me!

    (MYSHKIN exits.)

FERDYSCHENKO: You see, he's set the poor darling on fire. She's running mad with salvation. I told you I knew the type. Follow precedent, I say. Pour vinegar into him and nail him to a cross.

Scene Eleven

ROGOZHIN's Room

Lights up. MYSHKIN enters the room and looks around. ROGOZHIN appears.

ROGOZHIN: Well, Prince.

    (Laughs.)

    You've come to see me then?

MYSHKIN: You've been expecting me, Parfyon. Haven't you?

ROGOZHIN: Oh, I knew you'd come. Yes, I knew you'd come.

MYSHKIN: Outside - as I came to your door - I felt somebody's eyes - watching me.

ROGOZHIN: Did you, Prince? Somebody's eyes, eh?

    (Laughs.)

    Still, you got here alright, eh? That's the main thing. You're here now, aren't you?

MYSHKIN (after a pause): Where is she, Parfyon?

ROGOZHIN: Hiding. From both of us, Prince.

    (Laughs.)

    But I'm watching her, I'm watching. You won't have her again, Prince.

MYSHKIN: Parfyon - I'm not in love with her. I never have been. But I love her - because - because I pity her. Parfyon, listen to me, please, if you two go on together it will kill you. I care for both of you - for you too, Parfyon. Leave her alone, for your own sake!

ROGOZHIN: And do you pity me, too?

(Laughs.)

I've been hating you, Prince, all the time you two have been praying and talking and weeping together, I've been hating you.

MYSHKIN: Do you hate me now, Parfyon?

ROGOZHIN (after a pause, shakes his head): But pity for her - there's none of that in me, not a drop. She hates me, you see.

MYSHKIN: But don't you understand? She's ill. She's desperate - Parfyon, for the love of God.

ROGOZHIN: For the love of -

(Shouting.)

- she's in here, don't you see, Innocent!

(Strikes his forehead.)

Here!

(His chest.)

Here! and here and here.

(Strikes his knees savagely.)

I make myself into a dog for her sake, and she belongs to me as - as a master belongs to a dog.

MYSHKIN (stands looking at him hopelessly): Perhaps even so God will help you.

(Pause.)

I can't do anything more, Parfyon. If she comes back to you, I won't interfere. Not now.

ROGOZHIN: Won't you? Just by breathing you interfere. Look - at this painting - tell me -

(He lights the candle under Holbein's Christ.)

- do you believe in him?

MYSHKIN: Yes, but not like that. That is the picture of a man in despair - not the son of God. It could make us lose our faith.

ROGOZHIN: But you have faith.

(Nods.)

Do you have faith for me? For a man like me?

MYSHKIN (stares at him): Yes! Yes! There is faith everywhere in our country. I heard the story of a man who killed his best friend for a silver watch. And while he was doing it, cutting his old friend's throat, he cried out 'Oh God forgive me, brother, for Christ's sake!'

ROGOZHIN: Yes, that's faith, that's a man of faith!

MYSHKIN: And then on my way home a man - he was a drunken soldier - and he - look -

(Fumbles inside his shirt, shows a cross.)

- sold me his own cross for thirty copecks - a special silver cross he said it was.

ROGOZHIN (looks at it, laughs): It's tin.

MYSHKIN: Yes, I know. But it made me want to cry, Parfyon. For our country. Our Russia - there is faith here - the man who sold me this had faith.

ROGOZHIN: Here - here -

(Laughing, fumbles out his own cross.)

- take this -

(Forces his cross on MYSHKIN.)

- it's gold - good gold - now give me yours.

MYSHKIN: But yours is valuable.

ROGOZHIN: Yes, yes - come on.

(Holds out his hand.)

Please.

(They exchange crosses, MYSHKIN reluctantly.)

There, now we are brothers. Will you be blessed as my brother.

MYSHKIN: Yes. If you want it.

ROGOZHIN: Wait - wait here.

(Goes out.

MYSHKIN stands, waiting, begins to realise he is about to have a fit.

ROGOZHIN enters, holding his mother's arm. She is very old and blind. He leads her across to MYSHKIN.)

Mother, this is a great friend, a man I love as a brother. I've exchanged crosses with him, mother. Bless him as your son.

(MRS ROGOZHIN stands shakily, then raises her hand.

MYSHKIN kneels.

MRS ROGOZHIN mumbles incomprehensibly, makes the sign of the cross over him.

MYSHKIN gets up, helped by ROGOZHIN.

ROGOZHIN kneels.

MRS ROGOZHIN repeats the performance.

ROGOZHIN then leads his mother out.

MYSHKIN crosses the room in a daze, knocks over the card table.

ROGOZHIN steps into the room. Blows out the light under the Holbein. Turns, smiles at MYSHKIN, then raises his hand. There is a knife in it.)

MYSHKIN (in a whisper): Parfyon!

ROGOZHIN: Forgive me, brother, for Christ's sake!

(Raises the knife.)

MYSHKIN: Parfyon, Parfyon - don't -

(Whispering, then as ROGOZHIN advances he throws his arms out, begins to shake, throws his head back peacock-like, crashes to the floor, lets out a series of screams.

ROGOZHIN drops the knife, bends down, over MYSHKIN's head.)

ROGOZHIN (in horror): He's smiling, he's smiling! Get him away from me!

CURTAIN

ACT TWO

Scene One

The Park

During the interval the lights come up on a park in Pavlovsk, on an early summer's afternoon. There is a bench. There is a little group, picnicking, singing, talking, etc; a more elegant couple walk past talking, etc; prone on the grass, with a guitar beside him and a handkerchief over his face, is FERDYSCHENKO, also reading a newspaper.

From fairly close by a band is playing music. As the interval comes to an end, some of the people wander off the stage, and FERDYSCHENKO gets swiftly up, moves to the bench and appropriates the rest of the picnic.

Lights down.

FERDYSCHENKO: Ah, -

(Stretches.)

- isn't it lovely? So verdant, so tranquil! How nature refreshes our parched souls, coaxes them to send forth new buds - revives our sense of wonder, our joy in life! Eh!

(As a middle-aged COUPLE come by.)

Afternoon, Admiral, dear lady, welcome to Pavlovsk!

(The COUPLE look at him, ignore him.)

Well, he looks like an Admiral! Pavlovsk is full of Admirals, Generals, in early summer. They come out with the flowers. General, how d'you do, sir!

(As a military-looking GENTLEMAN saunters by, looks at FERDYSCHENKO with distaste, nods stiffly, and off.)

Aren't the odours of Pavlovsk intoxicating, it's summer, sir, summer - Pavlovsk, I love you. We all come here, you see, every year, after the St Petersburg winter, winters of darkness, of cold, of death - we free our little wings from ice, those of us who have survived, and flutter giddily to Pavlovsk, to get ourselves warm again. Ah, now here is a General's dear lady -

(As MRS YEPANCHIN backs on to the stage, accompanied

by ALEXANDRIA.)

- with one of her dear daughters, doubtless still a virgin.

MRS YEPANCHIN: I really don't see why we can't all keep together. It's very irritating -

ADELAIDA (smiling): Well, they want to talk, mother.

MRS YEPANCHIN: And so do I! Don't let her dawdle, Prince -

(Calling out.)

- you see we'll miss the band...

(PRINCE SHULOVSKY and ADELAIDA come on to the stage, SHULOVSKY holding ADELAIDA's arm.)

SHULOVSKY: I'm terribly sorry. It's my fault. I made her stop to look at the ducks.

MRS YEPANCHIN: Ducks!

(In astonishment, then smiles.)

Really. Come on, come on!

(MRS YEPANCHIN and the girls laugh.)

FERDYSCHENKO: Afternoon. Welcome to Pavlosk.

SHULOVSKY (as they exeunt): Does one know that fellow?

FERDYSCHENKO: Just say that the fellow knows you, sir.

(Calling after him.)

Hah! Here come the other gentlemen from Moscow, they come in pairs, you know, especially when there are sisters about -

(Picks up the paper, pretends to read as.)

AGLAYA: Mother will be very cross. She'll come looking for us, and then you'll be embarrassed.

RADOMSKY: No, don't let's go. Not for a minute. It's quite difficult to embarrass me, I promise you.

AGLAYA: Yes, I know. You're very gifted, Mr Radomsky.

RADOMSKY: No, I'm not at all gifted.

AGLAYA: Well then, perhaps you don't need to be - which is even better.

RADOMSKY (laughs): Well, I must say, I'd like a gift or two at

the moment. A lack of something or other is making me
feel I might as well go back to Moscow. And it's oppressively
hot there at this time of year.

(Staring at her, smiling intensely.)

Should I go?

AGLAYA: Yes, if you like Moscow when it's oppressively hot.

RADOMSKY: But then I should miss so much.

AGLAYA: Should you? Should you really?

(Suddenly serious.)

May I go for a walk, please?

RADOMSKY: Of course.

AGLAYA: No - by myself.

RADOMSKY: Oh - well - in the - here, do you mean? Whatever
would I tell your mother?

(Laughs.)

It would be slightly embarrassing -

AGLAYA: Then I've done something quite difficult, haven't I?

(Goes off.)

RADOMSKY (stares after her): Damn the girl!

(Saunters over to the bench to sit down, notices FERDY-
SCHENKO, who is still reading the paper.)

FERDYSCHENKO (from behind the paper): Good afternoon, sir.

(RADOMSKY turns, looks at him, looks away.)

Have you read this? Most absorbing -

RADOMSKY: What?

(Irritably, looks at the newspaper, which FERDYSCHENKO
is offering to him, while indicating a particular item.)

It's not a paper I particularly care -

FERDYSCHENKO: Oh, quite, quite, I know what you mean.
Scandalous, libellous, vicious - and this attack on a good
man - a kind man - and a friend of the Yepanchins, too.
Particularly Miss Aglaya - didn't I have the pleasure of
seeing you with Miss Aglaya -

RADOMSKY: What? An attack on –

(Takes the newspaper.)

ᵀERDYSCHENKO: Oh, wasn't that Miss Aglaya... there.

(MRS YEPANCHIN returns, looks around, makes an
irritable exclamation. RADOMSKY sees her, looks at
FERDYSCHENKO, turns. As he does so MRS
YEPANCHIN goes off. YEPANCHIN enters.)

YEPANCHIN (come on): Ah, there you are!

(To RADOMSKY.)

Where's everyone else?

RADOMSKY: I really don't know. In fact I scarcely know where
I am myself.

YEPANCHIN: Never mind, I know where they'll end up – come
along with me.

RADOMSKY: May I? Because, you know, I really would rather
like a chat with you about something – something close to
my um –

YEPANCHIN: My dear fellow – my dear fellow – feel free. I'm
at your service.

(Turns to go off with RADOMSKY.)

FERDYSCHENKO: Hey, General! General! We haven't seen
each other since that magnificent night at Nastasya Filippovna's, the night you got your necklace...

YEPANCHIN (looks at FERDYSCHENKO, turns, and hurries
off with RADOMSKY): – Nowhere's sacred these days –

FERDYSCHENKO: Ah, he's at it again! Collecting himself sons-
in-law; what a dedicated father! But it's Pavlovsk, Pavlovsk
that does it! Little murmurs of romance, delicate intrigues,
husbands in the offing, dowries in the air, ah, Russia, ah,
summer-time.

(Going off, stops.)

Scene Two

The porch

MYSHKIN appears on the porch, stretches out his arms, smiles.
LEBEDEV is sitting on the porch, reading a newspaper, chuckling,
becomes aware of MYSHKIN.

MYSHKIN: Aaah, isn't it beautiful?

(Smiles down at LEBEDEV.)

What are you reading?

LEBEDEV: Oh, just some nonsense - nonsense - brilliantly
written but -

(Gestures, putting the newspaper into his pocket.)

MYSHKIN: But don't stop for my sake, please.

LEBEDEV (gives an odd laugh): Permit me to bring you something, Prince? Some tea? Rugs? You'll need some rugs...

MYSHKIN (laughing): No, I shan't. I shan't need tea or rugs.
Look at me, Lebedev. Now how do I look?

LEBEDEV: A trifle better, your honour, on the way to being on
the mend - but a sudden wind or a cold stomach -

MYSHKIN: And how did I look when you first brought me here?

LEBEDEV: I'm not denying there's been a distinct improvement,
your Highness, since you first honoured my little cottage
with your um, tenancy, in as much as you were then without the use of your limbs, were mostly half-conscious.
But I maintain you're not up to any little business matters
as yet, won't be for a while, and as far as I'm concerned
there's no hurry.

MYSHKIN: Business matters?

(Bewildered.)

Oh dear, my poor Lebedev - the rent! Oh, please forgive
me - of course I'm up to it.

LEBEDEV: No no no no -

(Wags his head.)

- it's not even to be mentioned just yet. It's just that as
this house is only let out to me on a financial basis -

GANYA (appears in the garden, comes up the steps, he and MYSHKIN embrace): Happy birthday, Prince! Or had you forgotten?

MYSHKIN (shyly): No, no, I hadn't - I - thank you, Ganya, I hadn't.

(Laughing.)

LEBEDEV: I didn't know it was -

(Comes over, shakes MYSHKIN's hand.)

- happy birthday, Prince, happy birthday.

MYSHKIN: Look, do you know -

(Hurrying on.)

- there's poor old Lebedev, I mean, we haven't even <u>talked</u> about the rent after three and a half weeks.

GANYA (turns, looks at LEBEDEV): The rent?

MYSHKIN: Dear Lebedev -

(Gives him a hug.)

LEBEDEV: I wouldn't debase your birthday by even thinking of talking about the rent.

GANYA: Certainly not again, anyway.

(Little pause.)

Lebedev and I talked about the rent on the day he moved you into the house. We talked about it two months ahead.

LEBEDEV: Yes, yes, I believe you're quite right, quite right, there was some -

GANYA: Money.

LEBEDEV: Yes. Mr Ivolgin is absolutely to be trusted in this, sir, he'll clear everything up with you.

(Hurries inside.

MYSHKIN looks at GANYA very solemnly, then suddenly bursts out laughing.)

GANYA (after a moment, smiles): It's all very well, but he takes advantage -

MYSHKIN: But he gives us pleasure! Look how much pleasure he gives us. Well -

(Little pause.)

- what's the news today? Mmm?

(Smiling.)

GANYA: No news.

(Little pause.)

I just wanted to be the first to call by. To wish you a happy birthday.

MYSHKIN: I don't know what I'd have done without you. You've saved my life. If - if - Ganya -

(Shrugs.)

Ganya, if other people should drop in, well, why don't you stay and - and - you always hurry off, you know, and I'd hate to think you were too busy on my account.

GANYA (embarrassed): That's very delicate of you, Prince.

(Smiles at him affectionately.)

But actually I do have a number of letters - we'll see. Um, by the way, there's something I ought to mention. But it's nothing serious - have you seen a newspaper today?

MYSHKIN: No. No, I scarcely ever see the newspapers. But I can get you one - Lebedev had one -

GANYA (relieved): No, no - I don't want to see one, I loathe the things. Full of malicious gossip. It doesn't really matter. But what I do have to do is get your your signature - here -

(Opens his brief-case, takes out a few documents, hands him a pen.)

- for these, evidence against a few ludicrous claims on your inheritance. Mr Pavlischev's estate.

MYSHKIN: Claims?

GANYA: What?

(Laughs.)

Oh, I can assure you, Prince, that nobody inherits a rouble in Russia without receiving thousands of claims. There - there - you sign -

(Indicates.)

MYSHKIN (takes the pen): Well... -

> (Doubtfully.)

> - very well, um...

> (Signs.)

FERDYSCHENKO: Ah, there's a man of responsibility, a man of affairs, of position, of friends, a Prince indeed, a Sun-Shine Prince! Look how he smiles. Where's his winter now? Such God loves and will protect!

> (During this AGLAYA has come around the corner of the garden, is looking up at MYSHKIN and GANYA, as MYSHKIN finishes signing, then GANYA reaches for the letters.)

AGLAYA: Well? May I come up, then? Or are you too busy, and should I go away?

MYSHKIN (turns. GANYA also): Aglaya!

GANYA (bows briefly to AGLAYA, who smiles at him knowingly): Excuse me -

> (Takes the letters from MYSHKIN's hand.)

> I must get these off straight away.

> (Puts them into his brief-case, shuts it.)

MYSHKIN: Oh, Ganya - don't go.

GANYA: I really must - um -

> (Moves to exit.)

> - excuse me -

> (Glances quickly at AGLAYA, goes off.)

MYSHKIN: Ganya cares so much about my interests that I'm sure he's neglecting his own.

AGLAYA: Our experience of Ganya was that he could generally look after his own interests best when he was also looking after other people's. Do you find him a good secretary?

MYSHKIN: He's a very good friend.

AGLAYA: I expect that's because you're good to him. Mother thinks you're so good, that we should all grovel to you. In fact she's having some people in tomorrow, especially to meet you. Do you think she'll want them to grovel to you? They are quite important.

MYSHKIN: I'm sure they won't.

AGLAYA: But will you come? You don't have to.

MYSHKIN: Do you want me to come?

AGLAYA: Oh, you might as well, I suppose. But if you do, would you please be careful. The conversation might turn to a serious subject, so would you please refrain from joining in with tales of donkeys. And also we've got a very precious vase, so...

MYSHKIN: So you would like me to sit as far away as possible.

AGLAYA: So if you can be as unlike yourself as possible, it would be pleasant to see you. Happy birthday, Prince. Are you pleased it's your birthday?

MYSHKIN: I think – I think it's going to be the happiest birthday I ever had.

AGLAYA: At breakfast this morning Mother said I was to give you a special present. I'm to stop being rude to you.

MYSHKIN: I don't mind your being rude to me. In fact, I think it would make me nervous if you stopped.

(Laughing.)

AGLAYA: Well, I have stopped. Are you beginning to feel nervous?

MYSHKIN: Yes, I am.

(Laughing.)

But I don't mind that either.

AGLAYA: Then you must be quite well again. Are you?

MYSHKIN: I don't think I shall ever be ill again. Ever.

AGLAYA: Am I allowed to ask you a question, then?

MYSHKIN: Yes.

(Little pause.)

You've already asked me quite a few.

(Laughs.)

AGLAYA: But can I ask you any question I like, without upsetting you?

MYSHKIN (suddenly serious, looks at her): Yes.

(Anxiously.)

Um, what about?

AGLAYA: All the time you've been recovering, the whole of
Pavlovsk's been talking about you. I mean, about you and
Nastasya Filippovna. Have you been waiting for us to
mention her?

MYSHKIN: I'm very grateful that you haven't.

AGLAYA: Are you grateful because you're embarrassed? Or
ashamed?

MYSHKIN: I'm not ashamed. I'm not. There was nothing - nothing
shameful in what I did, or in what she - why she came to
me. Nothing.

(Pause.)

Aglaya, it was - it feels as if it were a long time ago. It was
in the cold, and in St Petersburg, and now - now it's summer
and I'm here - and Pavlovsk is so beautiful. When I think
about her it's only to hope that she's as happy as I am. I
pray that she is. But I can't help being happy myself, can I?

AGLAYA: Why are you so happy?

MYSHKIN: Because I feel as if my life is starting all over again.
What happened in St Petersburg, that was before my life
started.

(Little pause.)

And - and Aglaya - are you happy?

AGLAYA: Oh yes. Mr Radomsky's just asked me to marry him.

MYSHKIN: Oh. That's - that's - I haven't met Mr Radomsky, but
he always sounds - sounds -

AGLAYA: Delightful. Everybody says so. That's why he sounds
it. I expect he and father will try and arrange everything
very quickly. People will want me to marry him, you see,
especially as Adelaida is going to marry Prince Shulovsky.
Our weddings will be very famous.

MYSHKIN: Oh.

(Looks at AGLAYA, who turns away.)

FERDYSCHENKO (strums a few notes on his balalaika): Ah,
how sweet the pain they're sav-our-ing... In a few hours she

might belong to <u>another</u>! Ah, if only he would speak - but can he? Can he? My Prince - my Prince -

(As MYSHKIN takes a pace forwards.)

- a word, a word will do it! For God's sake.

(As MYSHKIN takes another step forward.)

MYSHKIN: Aglaya -

MRS YEPANCHIN: Ah!

(Comes sweeping into the garden, followed by PRINCE SHULOVSKY, ADELAIDA, ALEXANDRIA.)

There you are, you see - I told you she would be - what are you up to? Slipping away to torment the Prince - or have you remembered your promise for his birthday? Why do you always have to be first in everything -

(As she talks, has come over, taken MYSHKIN by the shoulders, now gives him a smacking kiss.)

Happy birthday, Prince, happy birthday, my dear, we were all going to come over together but the General went off in one direction, and she - but you don't look well!

MYSHKIN: No, I'm very well, very well, thank you.

AGLAYA: Mother doesn't think you're yourself unless you're ill. She prefers sick people.

MRS YEPANCHIN: We'll have absolutely no nonsense from you on the Prince's birthday, thank you.

(To MYSHKIN.)

She hasn't been nice, has she?

MYSHKIN: No no, she's been very nice -

MRS YEPANCHIN: You'd say that if she'd put you on your death-bed. Well, come on, you two, what are you waiting for?

ADELAIDA: Happy birthday, Prince. Happy birthday.

(Embraces him.)

ALEXANDRIA: Happy birthday, Leo Nikolaievich.

(Also embraces him.)

MRS YEPANCHIN: And you too, Prince Shulovsky.

SHULOVSKY: Happy birthday, Prince.

(As SHULOVSKY, laughing, gives MYSHKIN a hug.

MYSHKIN is also laughing.)

MRS YEPANCHIN: Yes, you do look quite well, after all. And
to think that when we heard that that awful Mr Lebedev -

(Sees LEBEDEV, who has appeared ingratiatingly on the
porch.)

- that kind Mr Lebedev had brought you here and came
around to see you, you <u>were</u> on your death-bed. Yes, he
was, don't laugh! We didn't know where he was or what he
was up to and suddenly he was on the other side of Pavlovsk
and on his death-bed. Isn't it true?

MYSHKIN: It is true. And I would have died if you hadn't made
me live.

MRS YEPANCHIN: Piffle! I merely made sure Mr Lebedev gave
you hot soup instead of cold. It was all that gallivanting
around St Petersburg that made you so ill. Oh, we know
all about it - or most of it, anyway.

(YEPANCHIN and RADOMSKY appear, walk towards them.)

And where have you been?

YEPANCHIN (slightly embarrassed): Why - just strolling here,
my dear. And happy birthday, Prince, happy birthday.

(Shakes his hand, then gives him a hug.)

And may I present - this is Mr Radomsky - from Moscow.

(Laughs.)

To tell you the truth, he was a bit shy about meeting you.

(As MYSHKIN and RADOMSKY shake hands.)

RADOMSKY: Well, I've heard so many good things about you -
I've felt quite awed.

MRS YEPANCHIN: Well then, you needn't have worried - the
Prince is far too clever to let anyone be awed by him.

YEPANCHIN: There you are you see - I told you - he's a great
favourite here.

MYSHKIN: Everyone is so kind to me. So kind. All my friends
- and Mr Radomsky, I hope we'll be friends, too - I -
I -

(Shakes his head.)

- but please, please, are you comfortable - are there enough seats - and we shall have tea, Lebedev, may we have tea?

(LEBEDEV hurries inside as MYSHKIN hurries about, making sure everyone is comfortable.)

There - you know people say such nice things about me -

(Everyone is now placed except MYSHKIN, who stands, smiling around.)

I'm sure I can't live up to them all.

BURDOVSKY (crash. Off): Swindler! Fraud! Swindler!

KELLER (off): Remember the student Burdovsky! Remember Burdovsky!

IPPOLIT: Justice! Justice from the idiot! Idiot! Idiot!

YEPANCHIN: Good God!

SHULOVSKY: What's that? What's that?

RADOMSKY (laughs): Good grief!

(LEBEDEV appears on the porch step.)

BURDOVSKY (off): Where's the idiot, Myshkin!

KELLER (off): Come out and face us, sir!

IPPOLIT (off): Justice, justice, justice!

MRS YEPANCHIN: What _is_ happening? Will somebody please explain -

LEBEDEV: Louts, madame! That is to say, students.

MRS YEPANCHIN: Students!

RADOMSKY: Do you mean, anarchists?

LEBEDEV: Anarchists!

(To a background of.)

KELLER (off): Follow me, sirs, we'll find him!

BURDOVSKY (off): Around here! This way!

MRS YEPANCHIN: Anarchists! Anarchists!

LEBEDEV (hurrying inside): Anarchists, madame! After the

Prince's blood! Which I shall defend –

MRS YEPANCHIN: Prince, do you know what those creatures want?

MYSHKIN: No, no, I don't!

SHULOVSKY: We must keep calm. If we keep calm they'll go away! I've heard they always do.

RADOMSKY: Do they, Hector. Well, that's a relief!

(They all turn towards the porch as.)

LEBEDEV (off): Well, louts, where are you? Where are you? Anarchists!

(BURDOVSKY, KELLER and IPPOLIT come around into the garden, look at the company's backs.)

MYSHKIN: If they want to talk to me, I shall be –

LEBEDEV (off): Off with you, I say!

MRS YEPANCHIN: Don't you say a word to them.

RADOMSKY: Sshh! They've stopped shouting.

SHULOVSKY: There. I told you they'd go away.

LEBEDEV: That's settled then. The cowards have...

IPPOLIT (clears his throat, coughs): Justice! We demand justice!

(The company swings around, as.)

BURDOVSKY and KELLER: Justice, justice for Burdovsky!

LEBEDEV (hurrying down the steps): How dare you come here! How dare you come to my house!

SHULOVSKY: Off with you! Go away, go on!

IPPOLIT (simultaneously): Justice, madame, justice!

KELLER (simultaneously): For Burdovsky! Burdovsky must be heard!

MYSHKIN: Please – please – gentlemen – please, if I can help, I am the – I am Prince Myshkin. You want to see me?

IPPOLIT: Ah! Prince Jesus. We want justice for Burdovsky!

KELLER: As a man of honour I demand –

BURDOVSKY: Justice, justice, justice!

MYSHKIN: But I - I don't understand -

KELLER: Justice for Burdovsky! Justice for Burdovsky.

MRS YEPANCHIN: <u>What is Burdovsky</u>?

KELLER: He is Burdovsky!

RADOMSKY (laughs): So it's justice for yourself -

BURDOVSKY: For myself!

(Laughs.)

I demand justice for the son of Pavlischev!

MYSHKIN: What? Pavlischev? Did you say Pavlischev?

BURDOVSKY: For the son of Pavlischev!

MYSHKIN: But Mr Pavlischev had no son! He never - I'm sure he didn't -

MRS YEPANCHIN: What are they talking about? Pavlischev's son, who's -

RADOMSKY: And where is this son of Pavlischev?

IPPOLIT: There!

(Points to BURDOVSKY.)

BURDOVSKY: I am Pavlischev's son!

YEPANCHIN: But I thought he was Burdovsky!

MYSHKIN: You - you - you say you are Pavlischev's son!

BURDOVSKY: I am Pavlischev's bastard! The serf-seducer's bastard.

MYSHKIN: No - no - you mustn't say that - Pavlischev couldn't - this is a terrible mistake. Mr Burdovsky please, what are you saying?

MRS YEPANCHIN: This is a mad house!

IPPOLIT: Of course.

(Laughs.)

That's how we knew <u>he</u> would be here.

KELLER: We are here for honour!

RADOMSKY: That generally means money.

BURDOVSKY: I say it again.

(To MYSHKIN.)

I am the serf-seducer's bastard.

MRS YEPANCHIN (simultaneously): Honour! What's that? What's that? Is it a uniform you're wearing? Is it? Is it?

(Suddenly rising and poking at KELLER with her umbrella.)

Well, speak up, officer, is it?

YEPANCHIN: My dear,

(Attempting to take her arm.)

I think –

MRS YEPANCHIN: Let go of me, I'm demanding an explanation of this soldier here, give it to me!

KELLER (fending off the umbrella): Madame, madame... I heard this young scholar's story in a bar –

(While simultaneously.)

MYSHKIN (to BURDOVSKY): Mr Pavlischev was a good man, a great man, a saint – he could never seduce – you say a seducer of serfs – he could –

BURDOVSKY: A saint! This saint of yours was a corrupter and seducer.

MYSHKIN: No, no, no. Why do you say this? What do you want? What do you want?

GANYA (who has appeared clutching his brief-case, laughs): Money!

(There is a silence, they turn to GANYA.)

They want your inheritance, Prince!

MYSHKIN: Ganya, thank God – there's some terrible mistake.

GANYA: I'm sorry, Prince. This is the preposterous claim I didn't want to bother you with. It never occurred to me that they would dare to show their faces –

BURDOVSKY: And who is this? May we have the honour of an introduction?

MYSHKIN: This is my good friend Ganya Ivolgin –

IPPOLIT: Oh, the secretary!

(Laughs.)

YEPANCHIN: A damned good one, in point of fact.

MRS YEPANCHIN: Yes, a very good secretary indeed. He'll deal with you.

BURDOVSKY: A damned good hireling. Well, hireling – this has nothing to do with you.

MYSHKIN: Please – please – gentleman – let me tell you about Mr Pavlischev – Ganya will tell you –

GANYA: I can tell you about them, Prince. This is a flagrant attempt by a trio of self-righteous swindlers –

KELLER (advances on GANYA): Sir, you realise what this means, I shall call you out, sir. I shall challenge you to a duel, sir. I shall call you out.

GANYA (laughs): So they find it easier to shoot me than to answer charges of grossly libelling the Prince.

MYSHKIN (to KELLER): The fault – if there is a fault – is mine. Please let me speak to you, all of you!

GANYA: But I frighten them, you see. What are you frightened of?

IPPOLIT: Frightened?

(Laughs contemptuously.)

Of a Prince's lackey?

GANYA: Why don't you sit down? Or are you afraid to sit down? Then let me ask you a few questions. It'll only take a moment. May I? May I?

BURDOVSKY (looks at him, then turns, whispers to IPPOLIT. Then folds his arms, sits down): Ask your questions, henchman!

MYSHKIN: Pavlischev could not seduce –

MRS YEPANCHIN: Prince! Mr Ivolgin, kindly ask your questions!

GANYA (in the silence): Mr Burdovsky, where were you born?

BURDOVSKY (grinning): Why, here in Holy Russia. I am a student, and my father was Leo David Pavlischev, your honour.

GANYA: And when?

BURDOVSKY: In 1841. I am a student and my father was Leo

David Pavlischev, your worship.

GANYA: 1841. And the month?

BURDOVSKY: July 18th, I am a student and my father –

GANYA (laughs): Was certainly <u>not</u> Leo David Pavlischev. As you've just established in front of witnesses.

(Taking a bundle of letters out of his brief-case.)

These are letters written by Mr Pavlischev in the month before, during and subsequent to that epoch-making event, your birth.

(Throws them into BURDOVSKY's lap.)

They establish beyond doubt that he was in Switzerland at the time.

(As BURDOVSKY picks up the letters, begins to go through them feverishly.)

I'm sorry, Mr Burdovsky, you may be a bastard, but you are not Mr Pavlischev's?

(Laughter.)

BURDOVSKY: This is a cheap – a cheap –

(Falters.)

Forgery.

(Begins to tear them up.)

GANYA: Tear away, my dear anarchists. They're only copies.

(Laughter.)

YEPANCHIN: Where did they pick the nonsense up in the first place?

RADOMSKY: Oh, doubtless from that nasty little newspaper. Unless they wrote the article themselves.

MRS YEPANCHIN: Do you mean to tell me this hateful – this spiteful rubbish has been printed. Where is it? Let me see it? What newspaper? What article?

YEPANCHIN: My dear, nobody would have a copy of that –

MRS YEPANCHIN: You then, you anarchists!

(LEBEDEV fishes his copy out of his pocket and offers it beamingly to MRS YEPANCHIN.)

IPPOLIT: We are not familiar with the landowners press.

MRS YEPANCHIN: Someone get me a copy.

(LEBEDEV steps forward to offer his copy.)

Thank you. Would someone be kind enough to read it to me. What's the matter with you all?

LEBEDEV (after a silence): Well, if madame insists.

AGLAYA: And does the Prince insist? Shouldn't we consult him, mother?

MYSHKIN: What?

(Bewildered.)

No, no, it doesn't matter, you see I think that these - these gentlemen really believed -

(IPPOLIT, BURDOVSKY, KELLER who have been muttering among themselves, now get up.)

MRS YEPANCHIN: Where are you going? Are you ashamed?

IPPOLIT: Ashamed?

MRS YEPANCHIN: I want to see your faces while I hear this. Read!

BURDOVSKY: Oh do you!

(Folds his arms, turns away. So does IPPOLIT.)

LEBEDEV (reading from the paper): Hail Myshkin, Prince of Mush-heads! and the subject of celebration verses throughout the land.

Sweet little Myshkin, for five years long
In an idiot's cloak was snugly laid.
Right he did not know from wrong,
And imbecilic games he played.
But home returning in gaiters tight,
He swipes a million from the dead,
Prays in Russia day and night,
And robs poor students of their bread.
But oh, Myshkin, noodle-head, corrupter of -

MRS YEPANCHIN (crying out): Stop it! Stop it! That's enough.

(Goes over, squeezes MYSHKIN's hand.)

So that's the kind of thing our student-anarchists write, is it?

RADOMSKY: Students of what, I wonder? It's scarcely literate.

MRS YEPANCHIN: Well which of you wrote it? Which?

LEBEDEV: Um, it's signed Liberator.

BURDOVSKY: We had nothing to do with that.

MRS YEPANCHIN: Didn't you? Didn't you? Do you expect me to –

IPPOLIT (laughs): He knows we didn't! He knows! Yes, because he knows who did! Look at the Jesus protecting his Judas. He needs him, you see, every Jesus needs a Judas.

(MRS YEPANCHIN turns on LEBEDEV.)

LEBEDEV: You promised me you wouldn't tell – you promised –

(To IPPOLIT as MRS YEPANCHIN advances, he ducks behind MYSHKIN.)

MYSHKIN: It doesn't matter, it doesn't matter, he can't help himself, he can't help himself.

MRS YEPANCHIN: Liberator! Liberator! Come here, Liberator!

LEBEDEV: Madame, madame...

MYSHKIN: Please, please, don't – don't – not for me – I don't mind, and – and – listen, Mr Burdovsky, I can tell you've had a hard life, and you were just misled, I know it – would you do me the honour, would you, of accepting a settlement of oh – ten thousand roubles!

MRS YEPANCHIN: What?

(Turning on him, outraged.)

IPPOLIT (laughs): Charity, charity – of course –

MRS YEPANCHIN: What – ten thousand – what – and you – you unspeakable – laughing!

(Turns on IPPOLIT.)

– although why shouldn't he, why shouldn't he, when he knows this – this –, will run after him with roubles. Won't you? Won't you?

MYSHKIN: Yes, if I have to.

MRS YEPANCHIN: Leave me alone.

(To YEPANCHIN, who has tried to take her arm.)

What will you do, _father_, while these – these – anarchist

lunatics set about pillaging our churches and stealing our
property and murdering your family before your eyes, and
what for? What for? What do you live for, anarchists and
lunatics, what? Not God! Not Christ! Not our Russia! No,
for infamy and violence and pain, and this, this, Prince, -
look at them, look at them, fool, look, are these the
people you want to crawl to and grovel for - how dare you
laugh at me, how dare you?

(IPPOLIT's laughter almost hysterical.)

AGLAYA: Mother - mother - you're shaming us!

MRS YEPANCHIN: Shaming. And who does this thing shame?

(Shaking IPPOLIT more violently as IPPOLIT's laughter
turns to coughing.)

MYSHKIN: He's ill! He's ill!

MRS YEPANCHIN: What? What? Oh - oh -

(As IPPOLIT collapses, coughing, she crouches beside him,
her hand to his forehead. MYSHKIN also.)

Oh, you poor boy, you poor poor boy, and to think I nearly
struck you, you shouldn't be up, you shouldn't -

(Gets up, looks around.)

Where is he? Liberator, come here!

LEBEDEV (steps forward, nervously bowing): Shall I fetch the
police...

MRS YEPANCHIN: Get this boy into a bed with fresh sheets. At
once!

(As LEBEDEV assists IPPOLIT up.)

And you two -

(To BURDOVSKY and KELLER.)

- what are you doing standing about like gentlemen while
this boy is dying - move -

(Watches as they lead IPPOLIT out.)

Don't worry, my dear, I shall be along to see you later on.

IPPOLIT (struggling): Let go of me, let me go, I'm here for
justice...

(Off.)

SHULOVSKY: So that's an anarchist, is it?

RADOMSKY: With his lungs in that condition, he certainly shouldn't be shouting all the time.

YEPANCHIN: Poor little devil...

MRS YEPANCHIN: He's a child. Just a child.

ALEXANDRIA: He looks so wasted...

MRS YEPANCHIN: You see, the Prince was quite right, after all. He -

(Takes his hand.)

- saw it at once and didn't want to harm him, if only we could listen to you instead of shouting at you, and on your birthday too.

AGLAYA (suddenly steps forward, announces in a loud, angry voice): I want to go home.

MRS YEPANCHIN: What?

AGLAYA: I have seen enough. I have seen enough goodness for one afternoon, and now I want to go home, please. Who will take me? Mr Radomsky, will you take me, please?

RADOMSKY: I would be delighted.

(To GENERAL and MRS YEPANCHIN.)

With your permission of course.

MRS YEPANCHIN: But, my dear, we're just leaving -

YEPANCHIN: Of course, of course - my dear, let the young things -

RADOMSKY: Thank you, sir.

(NASTASYA appears around the garden.)

NASTASYA: Eugene Radomsky - Darling! There you are! You are naughty! I've been looking for you everywhere.

RADOMSKY: I beg your pardon, madame, I really haven't the slightest -

NASTASYA (throws back her head, laughs): It's all right, it's all settled, we're quite safe now, I've fixed it with Rogozhin!

RADOMSKY: What? Rogozhin?

(Laughs, bewildered, looks around.)

NASTASYA: Yes, he's bought up every single I.O.U. , and you know how I can manage him. So you're in my power really, darling, do you object to that?

RADOMSKY: I.O.U.'s? I - really I -

NASTASYA (goes to him): Ah, ssssh, there's no need, not any more. But how splendid you look. I'm proud of you.

(She kisses him, turns, walks away, stops, and with her back to the company.)

I shall expect you tonight, of course!

(Commandingly, and goes out.)

RADOMSKY: She must be mad! I haven't the slightest idea what she means!

(AGLAYA looks at him, turns, walks off.

Laughs hopelessly.)

But look - Aglaya - really -

MRS YEPANCHIN: Good day, Mr Radomsky.

(YEPANCHIN glares at RADOMSKY, follows.)

RADOMSKY: It must be a joke of some kind -

SHULOVSKY (following the others out of the garden): Eugene, that was a bit -

RADOMSKY (turning to GANYA and MYSHKIN): Well - well -

(Then shouting angrily.)

- who the hell was she?

GANYA (with a sudden laugh): Why, that was Nastasya Filippovna, Mr Radomsky.

(Begins to walk down the steps, turns, looks at RADOM-SKY.)

Surely you've seen her somewhere before? She's mixed with some of the best society.

(Goes off.)

RADOMSKY (turns, looks at MYSHKIN, who is standing trans-fixed): Do you know, Prince - do you know -

(Laughs.)

I think I'm being victimized.

MYSHKIN: What?

> (Looks at him vaguely.
>
> RADOMSKY goes off.)
>
> What? Oh - oh - Not here! Not in Pavlovsk! It was so peaceful.
>
> (Walks to the day bed, sits down. As he does so, LEBEDEV comes out on the porch, looks at MYSHKIN, then walks over to him. He picks up a rug, goes over to him.)

LEBEDEV: Um, I was very, um, interested in your observation that, how did you put it? That I couldn't help myself, when we were discussing my little, um, literary effort. That was a wise and telling remark, sir, wise and telling and therefore just like yourself. When that scoundrel of a lawyer wrote asking me whether I'd be interested in doing a little piece about you, my instincts declared strongly against it. Strongly. But then I've always had an interst in the crusading kind of journalism and with seeing my name in print, it's been an ambition of mine, and you're quite right, sir, I couldn't help myself, any more than I can help turning on people without warning, lying over trifles, grasping at passing roubles, being frightened of my superiors, sir, um -

> (Bends down, puts the rug over MYSHKIN's leg.)

- I can't help it, sir, any more than I can help admiring and loving you more than any man - any man -

> (Pause.)

We've got that young trouble-maker in bed, sir, I've told those other two to keep his coughing down. Um...

> (Turns, goes inside.)

FERDYSCHENKO: So she's here, eh, Sunshine? And the sun's gone in, in Pavlovsk, eh? A nip of St Petersburg cold in the air again.

> (As MYSHKIN huddles under the blankets.)

Still, don't you worry, you huddle under your blankets, and keep your ears warm and your eyes shut and you snooze away, my idiot, because all will be well, all manner of things - Oh, sleep, little Myshkin sleep, my Prince...

> (NASTASYA enters as MYSHKIN, sleeping, is troubled with

a nightmare; she kneels on the step of the porch. MYSH-
KIN wakes and is startled by the sight of NASTASYA.)

NASTASYA: Do I frighten you? Are you frightened of me?

MYSHKIN: No, no, but - but please get up. Please.

(Helps her to her feet.)

NASTASYA: I had to see you again. Once more. Just once more.
Have I done wrong?

MYSHKIN: No, Nastasya. But what is it- when you came this
afternoon - what you did - are you unhappy? Can - can I
help you?

NASTASYA: Help me? You helped me as nobody else in the
world could have helped me. When I was wicked, when I
had no faith, when I was in despair and wanted only to die
- you told me to believe, you told me I could be good. Do
you remember?

MYSHKIN: I remember. Of course I remember, Nastasya. And
it was true. It was true. Didn't you believe me?

NASTASYA: I ran away from you because I believed in you.
Because I could never make you happy as you made me
happy. Because at last I understood something you were
trying to teach me. Listen, listen Leo Nikolaievich, you
taught me what love is. Love is being able to make people
happy. Isn't that right. Isn't it?

MYSHKIN: Making people happy - yes, yes, - that is a great
thing to do.

NASTASYA: A great thing! And you would make everybody
happy - you would love everybody - wouldn't you? But when
I heard that you were ill - that you might die- I prayed for
you and I watched over you, I had a spy to keep guard on
you for me -

MYSHKIN: A spy!

NASTASYA: Did you feel me near you in your illness, did you,
did you hear me praying that if you recovered I should find,
I, I should find some way of bringing you a great happiness
at last. I know I cannot be like you, Leo Nikolaievich I
cannot love everyone, but I can love you, I can make you
happy. Is that wrong?

MYSHKIN: No, Nastasya, it isn't wrong. You are good to want

that for me. I have always known you are good. But please, you must think of yourself, not of me. I am happy. I am already happy.

NASTASYA: I know. You remember one night in St Petersburg when you thought I was asleep, you came and sat by my bedside and you began to talk to me very quietly, as if you were in a dream, as if we were both in a dream. You talked of her. You'd only met her once, but you said she was so bright and quick and clear, like a light, an impatient angel.

MYSHKIN: Aglaya! But I wasn't - I was so confused. I'd only met her once and though she made fun of me, although she was cruel to me; it wasn't real cruelty. It was as if she had a vision.

NASTASYA: You said that if I met her, I would love her too. And now you are here in Pavlovsk, near her, and you have fallen in love with her. I know. I know. And that is why I have come to see you for one last time, Leo Nikolaievich. You must marry your angel. And though I shall never meet her, I shall love her, I love her already, because she will make you happy, yours will be a holy marriage that will bring me joy for the rest of my life.

MYSHKIN: No. No, no, Nastasya. You haven't understood. I - I - why Mr Radomsky - Aglaya and Mr Radomsky -

NASTASYA: Radomsky! Eugene Radomsky! Oh, my spy brought me here because of him.

(Laughs.)

He shan't have your Aglaya now.

MYSHKIN: You came for that!

NASTASYA: You see how powerful my reputation is. I can kill other people's with a smile. I killed Eugene Radomsky's reputation this afternoon.

MYSHKIN: Nastasya - Nastasya - oh, that is not right, that is not - that is not good. You must leave them alone, please. He loves her. He loves her. Leave them alone, for my sake!

NASTASYA: For your sake? Tell me that you do not love her, then?

MYSHKIN: I - I - I want her to be happy. Yes, I love her and I want her to be happy. That is what I want for her.

NASTASYA: She shall have her happiness, Prince. I shall give you both your happiness.

MYSHKIN: Nastasya - Nastasya - don't go - don't - listen, you must listen -

ROGOZHIN (who has been lurking U.S. throughout this encounter, suddenly appears as NASTASYA goes out): Well, brother?

(MYSHKIN takes a step back.)

Are you afraid of me, little brother?

(MYSHKIN shakes his head.

ROGOZHIN walks towards him, shows him his cross.)

See, I have it here still. Come here - come here and comfort me.

(Opens his arms.

MYSHKIN after a moment, goes to ROGOZHIN, ROGOZHIN embraces him.)

I have no knife. I shall never harm you again.

MYSHKIN: I know, Parfyon.

ROGOZHIN: And do you love her still?

MYSHKIN: Yes.

ROGOZHIN: And me? Do you love me?

MYSHKIN: Yes.

ROGOZHIN: Then do what she says, Prince. Marry. Marry the girl. Because when you are married and happy, Nastasya and I will be married. She's promised me that.

MYSHKIN: But you won't be happy, Parfyon.

ROGOZHIN: Oh, she didn't promise me that.

(Laughs.)

I never asked for that. But she came back to me even if it's you she loves, you she wants to see happy. So do what she says, Leo Nikolaievich, and we can go our separate ways. As brothers.

(Turns, begins to walk off.)

MYSHKIN: Parfyon.

(As ROGOZHIN stops.)

Help me! Tell her –

ROGOZHIN: Marry the girl!

(Shouting, goes off.)

FERDYSCHENKO: See, Prince, let us love you! A few months ago you were falling over yourself with love for everybody else, and now everybody else is falling over you with love. What's the matter?

(MYSHKIN has sat down on the day bed.)

Don't you like it? Don't you want other people to do unto you – eh?

(As RADOMSKY comes down the steps of the porch, while behind him, LEBEDEV, KELLER carry out a tray with glasses on, bottles.)

LEBEDEV: A party, Prince – a party for your birthday.

RADOMSKY: Happy birthday. Once again many happy returns, Prince.

FERDYSCHENKO: Let them love you! Let us love you!

(As RADOMSKY shakes MYSHKIN's hand.)

RADOMSKY: I just wanted to say, Prince, that I'm glad I met you this afternoon.

MYSHKIN: Thank you, Mr Radomsky. I – I wanted to say that I liked you very much. I hope we shall become friends.

RADOMSKY: I'm glad of that, because frankly I rather think I shall need your support, – I might as well admit it – everybody certainly knows by now anyway – there are a few I.O.U. 's – and Rogozhin has bought them up.

MYSHKIN: I'm – I'm terribly sorry. If I can help in any way –

RADOMSKY: Well, I should like you to know one thing, Prince. Whatever my past, I'm very much in love with Aglaya – I very much want her to be my wife.

MYSHKIN: Yes. I know.

RADOMSKY: Well – I'm very grateful for your friendship.

(Shakes hands again as.)

FERDYSCHENKO: Everybody loves you!

(Simultaneously, LEBEDEV, BURDOVSKY, KELLER appear.)

ALL: Happy birthday, Prince.

BURDOVSKY (shakes MYSHKIN's hand): You're a good man, Prince. I'm sorry for this afternoon.

FERDYSCHENKO: Loves you!

KELLER: An honourable man, sir!

(Shaking MYSHKIN's hand.)

FERDYSCHENKO: Loves you!

(LEBEDEV is filling glasses, passes them around.)

GANYA (hurries into the garden, goes to MYSHKIN, shakes him by the hand): Happy birthday, my dear Prince.

(FERDYSCHENKO starts on his guitar, a traditional birthday song.)

FERDYSCHENKO: Joy and Gladness. Joy and Gladness
Joy and Gladness fill your hearts, etc.

(Everyone joins in expect MYSHKIN, and then MYSHKIN also stands on the garden bench singing, laughing as he does so. The song ends with a burst of laughter and applause.)

MYSHKIN: My friends - my dear friends - how happy - how happy you make me!

IPPOLIT (appears on the porch through the door): Happy birthday, Prince! Happy birthday. Do you know what I've got here? A birthday present!

(Flourishes a manuscript, walks to the table, as they turn to look at him.)

MYSHKIN (goes over to him): Ippolit! But you shouldn't be up!

IPPOLIT: Why not? I shall soon by lying down -

(Coughs, checks himself.)

Well, Prince, shall I open it up - my confession and last words! My poor little biography, the conclusions of a short life.

FERDYSCHENKO: The life may be short, but the conclusions look long.

IPPOLIT: Or would it embarrass you to hear them?

(Flings it down on the table.)

My very last words, I can promise you that!

LEBEDEV (bustles in with a tray of food, plonks it down on top of the manuscript): Food, gentlemen!

(FERDYSCHENKO hurries over, begins to help himself.)

RADOMSKY: Food before revolution, it seems. May I?

(Goes forward, helps himself.)

KELLER: Come and have a bite, sir!

(Gives IPPOLIT a friendly pat on the shoulders as he joins the table, and so.)

IPPOLIT (set coughing again, watches them, then walks away from them, watched anxiously by MYSHKIN, surveys them contemptuously): It makes a splendid last view of the world, doesn't it, Prince?

(Turns, as if to leave.)

BURDOVSKY: Oh, Ippolit.

IPPOLIT: Burdovsky! What a splendid notion of justice. Feeding off millionaires.

MYSHKIN: Please - please don't go.

IPPOLIT: God, you disgust me!

(To all of them.)

But now at least I know what to do - without regrets! Without regrets!

MYSHKIN: Ippolit - Ippolit - what do you mean?

(Makes to follow, as.

IPPOLIT goes out.)

GANYA: Prince - Prince - don't worry. He's not going to do anything.

RADOMSKY: At least not until he's found a publisher for this.

(Pulls the manuscript out from under the tray.

FERDYSCHENKO takes it from him, with a laugh, begins to flick through it.)

MYSHKIN: No, no, I'm frightened for him.

BURDOVSKY: He means it, Prince. He's going to kill himself.
And he has the right.

GANYA: Kill himself - that egoist!

(Laughs.)

Not without an audience.

FERDYSCHENKO: I'll watch, with pleasure.

(Laughter.)

BURDOVSKY: You may laugh -

IPPOLIT (bursts to the porch): You will listen to me!

(Shouting.)

You will listen!

(Marches over, pushes the tray back, to get the manuscript,
stares down.)

Where is it? Give it back to me! Give it back!

(Hysterically, turning from person to person.)

FERDYSCHENKO: What are you searching for? Your conclusions?

IPPOLIT (faces FERDYSCHENKO, then laughs): It doesn't
matter. If it amuses you to play games with a - with a -

(Starts coughing.)

RADOMSKY (comes over, takes the manuscript from FERDY-
SCHENKO, hands it to IPPOLIT): You're quite right.
We're developing a nasty habit of contempt, in this country,
for our literature.

(IPPOLIT snatches it from him, then throws it on the floor.)

MYSHKIN: Please don't be angry, Ippolit.

IPPOLIT: Angry?

(Laughs.)

Angry? I came here to do one thing - one last act of justice
before I die, to remedy one evil, however insignificant, one,
that's all I could hope for. And what do I find? I find you!

(To MYSHKIN.)

The only man in Russia who hasn't the <u>wit</u> to commit an injustice!

MYSHKIN: I'm sorry, I –

IPPOLIT: Do you know that if it weren't for this – this–

(Slaps his chest.)

I could have been a good man, yes, a good man, a man who could do things to change the world, the laws, to help change our society. Because that, Prince, <u>that</u> is what goodness is! Not charity, and innocence and forgiveness but decision and action, the courage to be cruel! Without cruelty how else will it be done – the enthronment of the principle of justice! Justice! Justice through –

(Coughs.)

– action! Not –

(Coughing.)

– not all the filthy, corrupted feelings of a smirking Christ, you fool, what are you doing? What are you doing? Do you think you're gathering all the little children, suffering them to come unto you. Children! Look at your children, look at your vermin, your parasites and vermin.

(There is a silence. He draws himself up.)

It is an obligation to choose death in the company of you and your children. Do you understand. This –

(Slaps his chest again.)

– doesn't choose me. I choose death!

LEBEDEV: Drink, drinks, everyone –

(Seizing a bottle.

GANYA and RADOMSKY laugh.)

MYSHKIN: No, no.

(Rushes to IPPOLIT, who is leaving, catches his arm.)

What are you saying?

IPPOLIT: I have the right and I have a pistol.

LEBEDEV: What? Pistol?

(Runs over to IPPOLIT, grabs his other arm.)

Oh no, he doesn't have the right – I'm responsible for the condition of this house.

MYSHKIN: Ippolit, Ippolit, don't you see. It's not over yet, it's never over until the last. There are things you can do, you're right about justice, about action, but <u>you</u> must do it, you.

LEBEDEV: No, I'm sorry, Prince. I know the type. If he doesn't hand over the pistol, I shall send for the police.

IPPOLIT (stops struggling, smiles): All right, Prince, for your sake.

(To LEBEDEV.)

It's under the pillow on your bed.

(Laughs.

LEBEDEV hurries out.

To MYSHKIN.)

Yes, you really are a good man. You really do love. You're not evil, Prince.

(Pause.)

You're pathetic.

(Walks away from them.)

The sun will rise soon.

FERDYSCHENKO: Oh, for God's sake.

GANYA: Get him out of here.

IPPOLIT: I wanted to see the sun.

FERDYSCHENKO: Cock-a-doodle-doo!

(Puts his hand into his dressing-gown pocket.)

Just one more time, I wanted to see it.

(IPPOLIT whips the pistol out of his pocket, raises it to his head.)

LEBEDEV (returning): Very funny, come on now, where – ?

(Freezes.)

IPPOLIT: Keep back, keep back.

MYSHKIN (in a despairing whisper): Ippolit – Ippolit – now –

please –

(IPPOLIT pulls the trigger. There is a click.

FERDYSCHENKO, GANYA and LEBEDEV laugh.

IPPOLIT jerks frantically at the pistol as KELLER leaps down the steps, snatches it away from him. IPPOLIT struggles, then sinks to the floor.)

RADOMSKY: There's no firing cap.

(MYSHKIN crouches beside him, puts an arm around him.)

IPPOLIT: What? Wha-? Here, here it is – I forgot – give it back to me, please.

(Lunges for the pistol. KELLER restrains him.)

FERDYSCHENKO: Oh, don't be mean. Let him try again.

(BURDOVSKY, KELLER, lead IPPOLIT out, sobbing. GANYA and RADOMSKY, at first smiling coolly, begin to laugh. As the door closes behind IPPOLIT, the stage fills with laughter.)

MYSHKIN (stands staring around him in horror, then bellows): In God's name – in God's name –

(Then into the silence.)

You are being cruel! Why are you? Why?

(Stands, his mouth opening and closing.)

It's not – we mustn't be – we're – we're – aren't you ashamed? Aren't you?

(They stand in silence, then RADOMSKY goes to him, as if to say something, then turns, goes off. Then GANYA goes to him, puts his hand on MYSHKIN's shoulder.)

GANYA: Prince – Prince?

(After a moment GANYA turns, goes out.

LEBEDEV stands disconsolately, then goes inside.

MYSHKIN gets up, stares at FERDYSCHENKO, walks towards the steps, goes up, stands looking at FERDYSCHENKO, as if to say something, smiles, turns, goes up the steps and in.

FERDYSCHENKO goes on playing, then sings the song again, the words now audible.)

FERDYSCHENKO: Sweet little Myshkin, with so much love,
　　Bears his pain like a sucking dove,
　　But oh cruelty, cruelty wears him down,
　　And turns to thorns the lover's crown.

Scene Three

YEPANCHIN's party

Lights go up on the YEPANCHIN room.

Low buzz of conversation.

Present are: GENERAL and MRS YEPANCHIN; ALEXANDRIA;
ADELAIDA; PRINCE SHULOVSKY; GENERAL PETROVICH;
PRINCESS BELEKONSKY; ELDER STATESMAN, AGLAYA.
The three sisters are talking to PRINCE SHULOVSKY. The
door opens.

MRS YEPANCHIN: Of course my girls have never been abroad.
　　The General promised to take us to Switzerland in the Autumn.
　　But now that will have to wait on Adelaida and Prince
　　Shulovsky.

PETROVICH: He's a fine young man, and, may I say, a very
　　lucky one. She's a very fine young lady.

MRS YEPANCHIN: Thank you.

ELDER STATESMAN: Not that I was against the abolition. I
　　never was, never. But the rest of us have a right to justice,
　　and not just the serfs.

MRS YEPANCHIN: I only hope my Aglaya does as well.

PRINCESS BELEKONSKY: Has she given up that nonsense about
　　wanting an education? That won't do her any good.

FOOTMAN: Eugene Alexandrovich Radomsky.

　　(RADOMSKY with a smiling boldness, comes into the room,
　　goes over to MRS YEPANCHIN, offers his hand. MRS
　　YEPANCHIN takes it.)

RADOMSKY: I'm sorry - am I late?

MRS YEPANCHIN: Not at all. No - no.

　　(Slightly flustered.)

My dear –

(To YEPANCHIN.)

Here is Mr Radomsky.

(RADOMSKY shakes hands with YEPANCHIN.)

YEPANCHIN (also flustered): My dear fellow, um, how nice – um, Prince, here is Mr Radomsky, Prince.

(Takes him over to SHULOVSKY.)

RADOMSKY (to SHULOVSKY, and partly to AGLAYA): But you all look so surprised to see me.

AGLAYA: Mother said you'd probably had to go back to Moscow unexpectedly.

RADOMSKY: I think if I had gone back, it would have been quite expected.

SHULOVSKY: Anyway, we're glad you haven't. Very glad. Eh?

(To ALEXANDRIA.)

FOOTMAN: Prince Leo Nikolaievich Myshkin!

(MYSHKIN comes through the door.

YEPANCHIN comes over to him, shakes him by the hand.)

MRS YEPANCHIN: Ah! Prince. Count Chernevsky. Now here's the young man we've been telling you about, Princess Belekonsky. This is Prince Myshkin. The Princess is my Godmother.

(MYSHKIN takes BELEKONSKY's hand, bows.)

PRINCESS BELEKONSKY: You look extremely fit to me. They say you've been ill.

MYSHKIN: Yes, yes, I was, but I've recovered entirely, thank you.

MRS YEPANCHIN: General Petrovich – Prince Myshkin.

MYSHKIN (bowing, shaking hands): How do you do, sir.

(MYSHKIN smiles, puzzled. MYSHKIN shakes hands with ELDER STATESMAN.)

MRS YEPANCHIN: Now come and sit by General Petrovich, he was just telling us –

(Goes over to the tea urn.)

- that he knows lots about you.

MYSHKIN (going over to sit in the chair next to PETROVICH, sees the vase on the stand behind it, knocks the vase, clutches at it, to steady it): I'm sor–

MRS YEPANCHIN: He was related to your benefactor, Mr Pavlischev.

MYSHKIN: What? Who?

(Looks around.)

PETROVICH: I was.

MYSHKIN: Really, sir?

(Leans towards PETROVICH eagerly.)

A relative of Mr Pavlischev?

PETROVICH (laughs): Don't you believe me?

MYSHKIN: Yes – yes, of course. Forgive me.

(Glances quickly at AGLAYA.)

I mean – it's only that, well, in my view our Mr Pavlischev was a great man.

PRINCESS BELEKONSKY: Ah, you mean you're surprised that our General could be related to a great man?

MYSHKIN: I'm being stupid, aren't I?

(Also laughing.)

It's just that Mr Pavlischev is almost a – well, a kind of saint to me.

(Laughs, looks anxiously at AGLAYA, then goes over to sit in the chair next to hers.)

PETROVICH: Yes – yes – I always liked him. Must say. Very charming – very indeed.

ELDER STATESMAN: I remember Pavlischev – he was the chap who got mixed up with the abbé – er – the abbé – one of those abbés – I remember the noise it made.

PRINCESS BELEKONSKY: The Abbé Goureau, a Jesuit.

PETROVICH: That's right – cunning old fox Goureau – he had charm, I'll say that for him.

ELDER STATESMAN: There you are, you see - a man of good
   birth, Pavlischev, a Count Chamberlain, wasn't he?

   (Shakes his head.)

   Goes over to Catholicism, becomes a Jesuit and quite -

MYSHKIN: Pavlischev - Pavlischev - converted to Catholicism
   - a Jesuit - but it's impossible!

PETROVICH: Oh, old Abbé Goureau knew what he was up to, all
   right. Do you know the fellow had the nerve to put in a
   claim under the will -

MYSHKIN: But this is shocking - shocking!

   (Silence from the rest of the company. They look towards
   MYSHKIN, then resume as.)

PETROVICH: What! My dear Prince, you've been away too
   long. Why -

   (To PRINCESS BELEKONSKY.)

   - only last summer Princess Yegarin entered a Catholic
   convent. They've got a certain style, you see - really
   seductive preacher, Goureau, from all accounts.

ELDER STATESMAN: Well, it's no secret - they tried to get
   hold of me once in Vienna in 1832 - 33? - no, 32. Of
   course I was an innocent then.

   (Chuckles, nods at MYSHKIN.)

   But still, I had the answer, I ran away.

PRINCESS BELEKONSKY: With the Countess Levitsky, wasn't
   it?

ELDER STATESMAN: With the Countess, but from the Priest.

PRINCESS BELEKONSKY: Isn't it amazing? They boast of
   their conquests in their youth, and turn them into religious
   experiences in old age. While we -

   (To MRS YEPANCHIN.)

   - do just the opposite.

PETROVICH: Now you mention it, there was something
   womanish about that abbé of Pavlischev's - very soft
   shape, know what I mean? And a soft way of talking.

MYSHKIN: No! No!

(Again silence, all heads turn.)

Mr Pavlischev was a man of great intellect and a true
Christian - a believer. How could he - how could he have
been swindled into a superstition that's - why that's a
thousand times worse than atheism?

YEPANCHIN: I say, Prince, that's a bit, er, strong, old fellow.

MYSHKIN: A thousand times, a thousand thousand times -
Atheism merely preaches negation, but Catholicism teaches
a distorted Christ, an evil Christ. I tell you - I tell you
- when I was in Switzerland I read their books, their
sermons. Why, it isn't even a religion, it's a continuation
of an earthly throne defended by the sword and coloured
by blood - it has trifled with - it has trifled with -

(Looking around unseeingly.)

- the most sacred, truthful, innocent and desperate yearnings
of the people - yes, yes - by your words ye shall know
them it is written. I have read their words and they are
abomination.

ELDER STATESMAN: I must say, it makes a pleasant change
to meet a young man with religious feelings in this day
and age. Don't agree with you, mind. At least, I can't
go all the way -

YEPANCHIN: I think you're being a bit severe, Prince.

PETROVICH: Yes, I expect Pavlischev - well, he was a sick
man, you know, and perhaps a bit -

(Chuckles.)

- bored, eh?

MYSHKIN: Bored! Could a dying human be bored! Pavlischev
could not - unless he was past all - all - it is my con-
viction - I believe - I - I - I - am I am - a Russian - one
of our people - listen to me - <u>listen</u> - hear me -

(Stands up, voice rising.)

- we Russians have to understand - our salvation is here,
here in our homeland. I have been away so long, and I have
come back as if new-born, and I see, all around me, that
faith which is our homeland. That faith which is our real
homeland, shining forth to dazzle our eyes if we would
only look, look around us. Oh, do not talk, in God's name
of Jesuits, that they are seductive. Why, a Russian donkey

a simple Russian donkey. I once heard braying –

(There is a pause, he shakes his head, looks around at them, sees AGLAYA, who is staring at him with brilliant devotion.)

I – Aglaya – I –

(His elbow moves uncontrollably it hits the vase, the vase sways, crashes to the floor.

He looks at AGLAYA pathetically.)

PETROVICH: Oh, my God.

MYSHKIN (mumbling): Sorry, I'm sorry, Aglaya, forgive me, forgive me...

YEPANCHIN: Sergei –

(Gestures to FOOTMAN to clean it up.)

PRINCESS BELEKONSKY: I gave that vase to my God-daughter.

(Sternly.)

She has kept it there for ten years and she has hated it for ten years. And so have I. You have put us all out of our embarrassment, Prince.

AGLAYA: It's only a vase, Prince – only a vase.

RADOMSKY (amidst laughter): You see, Prince. Good will out.

AGLAYA (brings him a cup of tea, touches his hand): You see, Prince – it's all right – you see how much we all like you.

MYSHKIN (looks around joyfully): You've forgiven me? How kind you all are, how kind. And do you know, last night for the first time since coming home there was suddenly so much pain and cruelty and – and confusion that I thought – it was an evil thought – that perhaps even good could do harm, because... I seemed to have no tongue and all I could do was smile and cry out, because I thought that we were blind and we were deaf but really we're children – we're capable of being marvellously happy, and of being so good to one another if only we... if only we... but listen, later a man in the dawn began to sing a song to me – and I knew I could speak, listen, I knew I could ask how we can listen to a song and not be happy, how we can hear the birds –

(Gets up.)

- and not be happy. It is love, we must listen and we will hear it all around us, yes, here, here in our Russia, I am a Prince and I tell you this, there is love everywhere in our Russia, in railway carriages, in rooms like this, in the darkness, why! look at a child how it smiles, look at God's sunlight, how it changes the world to brightness every dawn, at the whole - at the whole -

(He is smiling, his body trembling, staring ahead.)

AGLAYA: Papa! Papa!

(Rising.)

MRS YEPANCHIN (also rising): Oh my God!

MYSHKIN (spreading his arms wide): - that moves by love - I - I -

(Crashes backwards to the floor.)

AGLAYA (whose arm is being held by RADOMSKY, breaks free, runs to MYSHKIN, kneels beside him, cradles his head): I - I - I -

(Draws MYSHKIN's head against her breast protectively.)

FERDYSCHENKO: Wasn't it touching, eh? To win your light, your angel, your virgin, by smashing the furniture, falling to the ground, foaming at the mouth, crying out that Christ was come again, to wit your idiot self? And what can an impatient Russian virgin do? - but grovel at your heels as they drum on the ground, and accept you, accept you before the whole world, foam and all? And then what? How do you improve on such a delicate piece of wooing?

(As lights go up on the porch, LEBEDEV standing, looking apprehensively in.)

Hey - how are the young things?

LEBEDEV: How do I know? He won't even go around and see her. He spends his nights sobbing and laughing and his days skulking inside or popping out to check on the birds, what's the matter with him, it's a magnificent match, magnificent!

FERDYSCHENKO: Why, man - that's not the tactic of an idiot. Come and have a drink - come on -

(As LEBEDEV comes down the steps, puts an arm around his shoulder.)

Don't you see – he's making her come to him –

(As they go off.)

– the ruthless devil Hey!

(As.

AGLAYA comes around into the garden.

MYSHKIN comes out on to the porch, sees AGLAYA, makes
as if to turn and blunder back inside. Then turns around
again.)

AGLAYA: I may come up and speak to you, may I?

(Comes up the steps.)

As you won't come to us. It was kind of you, though, to
answer enquiries after your health.

MYSHKIN: I'm sorry, Aglaya, I've wanted to come. But I've
been so ashamed.

AGLAYA: Ashamed?

MYSHKIN: You warned me – and I did all those things – the vase
– everything. Worse. Worse.

(Despairingly.)

AGLAYA: Yes, it was remarkable. You even managed a refe-
rence to donkeys. But it was very dramatic, I enjoyed it.

(Long pause.)

Well, haven't you anything to say to me?

MYSHKIN: Only that – I'm glad you've come.

AGLAYA: Thank you. I don't know whether I'm glad I've come
yet, or whether I'm being very stupid. Can you tell me?
Or are you very stupid too, and is that why you're so nice
and do funny things.

(Laughs.)

Mother doesn't know whether to laugh or cry, so she's been
doing both and scolding me, and father's out whenever he
can be, and Mr Radomsky hasn't been around once, and –
well, if you are going to say anything, you must say it
now? What is the time please?

MYSHKIN (fumbles his watch out, looks at it, replaces it): I
love you, Aglaya.

AGLAYA: Ah.

(As MYSHKIN comes over to her, turns, with her back to him.)

I love you too, Leo Nikolaievich.

MYSHKIN: Aglaya - Aglaya - I -

(Laughs.)

I've dreamed -

AGLAYA: And will we be happy together?

(Turning to him.)

MYSHKIN: I hope so. I pray so.

AGLAYA (gently): But how can we be happy, Leo Nikolaievich?

MYSHKIN: If we - if we love -

AGLAYA: But are you free to love me?

(MYSHKIN struggles to speak.)

You see, you don't know. Do you?

MYSHKIN: Aglaya - I - I - want to - marry you.

AGLAYA: Then you must tell me so, in front of her. You must tell me that you are free, in front of her.

(As NASTASYA comes around the corner, into the garden. But not yet seen. ROGOZHIN is with her.)

MYSHKIN: No, Aglaya - no, we must leave her alone.

(Sees AGLAYA, who has turned, and is looking at NAS-TASYA. Also turns.)

NASTASYA (comes up the steps, she is smiling): Well, are you happy now?

AGLAYA: Happy? Why do you ask that?

NASTASYA (still smiling): Haven't I the right to ask?

AGLAYA: Have you? Only if you think you have made us happy.

NASTASYA (after a pause, coldly): You sent me a note. You wanted to see me.

AGLAYA: I want you to answer my question, please. What have you to do with - with our lives?

NASTASYA: And that is why you sent for me?

AGLAYA: I have a right. I have a right to know why you have been pestering me.

NASTASYA: Pestering you.

AGLAYA: Pestering me. With your letters, for instance.

MYSHKIN: Letters? What - what letters?

NASTASYA: You didn't like receiving my letters, then?

AGLAYA (laughs, takes a number of letters out of her reticule): Like them? Listen, listen, Prince, listen, 'My darling Aglaya, I have never seen you properly, but how I long to talk to you. I love you, yes, I love you even as I know he loves you, because for me, as for him, you are perfection, an angel. Yes, an angel, because he loves you, and as I love him, I yearn for one thing only, one great thing in my life, and that is that you and he should be married. But I must not love perfection, I am not entitled to, yet how can I help loving -'

MYSHKIN: Aglaya, stop, stop this!

AGLAYA: But my spies have told me you already belong to each other in thought and feeling, and in my blessing - your blessing -

(Holds the letters out to NASTASYA.)

Would you take them back, please?

NASTASYA (without moving): I gave you offence then. I'm sorry.

AGLAYA: And what did you mean to do? Your blessing - you give us your blessing? What is your blessing worth, except to show that the Prince is yours, to give away? Am I to be grateful to you for making a present of him? Is that it?

(Throws the letter to the ground. Laughs.)

MYSHKIN: Aglaya, she didn't - she doesn't mean -

AGLAYA: Do you think I don't know? She's been going round boasting that she's been bringing us together.

(To MYSHKIN.)

NASTASYA: Who told you that?

AGLAYA: That she's going to sacrifice the Prince for my sake. How you were going to 'give him up' to me!

(MYSHKIN staring from one to the other, bends, picks up the letters, makes a vague gesture, as if offering them to first AGLAYA, then to NASTASYA as.)

NASTASYA: You are <u>very</u> disappointing. You know, I thought you'd be cleverer. But you're not even particularly pretty.

AGLAYA: Really?

(Laughs angrily.)

And do you think your opinion matters to me? Just because you offered yourself for sale at one of your disgusting parties, and he was so simple, and yes, good to be able to bear what you were doing and tried to stop you by pretending to love you, do you really believe he's yours, to give away?

MYSHKIN: Aglaya, for God's sake, you must stop!

AGLAYA: But all you really care about is your own disgrace, the thought that everyone knows what you've done, what you are, how dare <u>you</u>, <u>you</u> of all women, behave as if you have any rights - why don't you marry <u>him</u> -

(Points at ROGOZHIN.)

- at least he wants you, or so people say.

MYSHKIN (takes her arm): Oh, Aglaya - oh, Aglaya -

(Moaning.)

AGLAYA: If you'd ever really wanted to be an honest woman, why didn't you give up Mr Totsky and do some decent, common work, instead of turning yourself into a public joke! Why didn't you?

NASTASYA (laughs): His angel! A light! A little thing like you - a frightened little thing!

AGLAYA: Frightened? Of you?

(Also laughs.)

NASTASYA: Of course. You know he still loves me.

AGLAYA: He hates you. He pretends to worry about you, but he pities you.

NASTASYA: Does he? Do you think he loves you! You're less worthy of him than I am, you - you intolerable <u>child</u>. See what you've done to him. See. Is that what you brought me here for, to do this to him? Still, take him. Take your man!

(In a sudden scream.)

Take him!

(Pause.)

Because if you don't claim him now, you'll lose him forever. I shall order him –

(Nods.)

– order him to give you up. That's all I have to do. I shall order him to marry me, do you understand.

AGLAYA (to MYSHKIN): Tell her!

NASTASYA (laughs): You claim to love him and you don't understand anything – anything – about him. He suffers. You see, he suffers. He can't help you. You'll have to tell me yourself...

AGLAYA: Tell her!

NASTASYA: Please, what am I to do, Miss Yepanchin? Am I to let you have him? Or shall I have him? The choice is yours.

AGLAYA (in a whisper): Leo Nikolaievich, please!

NASTASYA: Very well. Prince, you may tell her this. Tell her that you love me and will marry me. Tell her now, please. She wants to know.

(MYSHKIN staring bewildered from NASTASYA to AGLAYA, gets up, looks to NASTASYA.)

AGLAYA: No!

(MYSHKIN looks at her blankly.)

No!

(Runs wailing off.)

MYSHKIN: Aglaya!

(Takes a step after her.)

NASTASYA: No! No!

(MYSHKIN turns to NASTASYA.)

Do you choose her?

(Pathetically, sways and begins to collapse into a chair.

MYSHKIN goes over to her, lowers her to the chair.

ROGOZHIN comes out of the shadows.

NASTASYA puts her arms around MYSHKIN, rocks back and forth with him, then in a child's voice.)

Are you really mine then? Are you? Are you?

MYSHKIN: Yes.

NASTASYA: Will you say it, please?

MYSHKIN: Really yours.

(In a mumble.)

NASTASYA (hugs him. Looks at ROGOZHIN): Go away. You're not wanted now.

(ROGOZHIN after a moment, turns, walks off.

NASTASYA clutching MYSHKIN begins to rock backwards and forwards.

Lights down.)

FERDYSCHENKO: Well, off with the new, on with the old. But the aristocracy of it! Who but a Prince of saintly lineage could switch fiancées in a matter of minutes and in the presence of both ladies. Ah, Pavlovsk - Ah, naughty intoxicating Pavlovsk - see how midst thy flowers, thy parks, thy shades - see how - young hearts come together, flounce apart, attach themselves elsewhere, all is balmy, all is young, all is fickle. It doesn't matter what couple end up at the altar as long as the simple folk of this verdant town have before them the prospect of Pavlovsk's wedding of the year!

(As LEBEDEV comes onto the porch.)

Hey - hey - how's our bridegroom - about to enter the gates of Heaven at last -

LEBEDEV: Shut up! Shut up!

FERDYSCHENKO: ... where many have passed in before, eh?

(Bows, laughs.)

He'll have to leave the other ladies alone now though, the rogue, the scourge of impatient virgins -

LEBEDEV: Shut up, I said. Filth!

(Advancing on him.)

It's bad enough without you...

FERDYSCHENKO (as he dodges off): Well, give him my love,
I'm off to speed the happy bride on her way... Joy and
gladness, and joy and gladness.

(Exits.)

RADOMSKY (appears, sees the tail end of this, and as LEBEDEV
turns and bows to him): Good afternoon. Is the Prince er,
is he um, um, um?

(LEBEDEV nods towards the inside of the house.)

And how is he?

LEBEDEV (angrily): Saintly! Saintly!

RADOMSKY: Of course.

LEBEDEV: They say there's a crowd gathering round Nastasya
Filippovna's house to send her off, so to speak. To the
church.

RADOMSKY: Yes, I'd heard.

LEBEDEV: Feeling's strongly against her. They don't like her.
Miss Aglaya's very popular in the town, and so's the Prince
- they don't like what that - that - what she's doing to him.
There'll be trouble.

RADOMSKY: Yes, I daresay.

LEBEDEV: And Rogozhin - he's turned up for the wedding.

RADOMSKY: Oh dear!

LEBEDEV (bursts out): And I know who's responsible, I've
worked it out -

(Taps his forehead.)

- in here, I know, I know who the spy is, who the traitor
is. It's all a plot, a vicious plot.

RADOMSKY: What? A plot - ?

(Stops as MYSHKIN comes out, dressed as for the wedding.

LEBEDEV goes past him, back inside, as MYSHKIN comes
down the steps.)

MYSHKIN: I was afraid you wouldn't come to see me again.

RADOMSKY: Good Heavens, Prince, we're friends, aren't we?

(Pause then laughs.)

Look, I know it's no consolation to a man like you, but Aglaya's turned me away - so she won't see me - she won't have anything at all to do with me, so at least the worse man hasn't won, eh?

MYSHKIN: Oh, I'm sorry. I'm truly sorry.

RADOMSKY: Yes, I'm sure you are. I knew you would be. Um look, I came to say something - you're really going to go through with it then?

(Laughing.)

It's offensive of me beyond - do excuse me - but -

(Laughs again.

MYSHKIN laughs also.)

I can't - I can't take it seriously. I really can't. There was no reason for Aglaya's jealousy, was there? None at all. You could have calmed her with a word.

MYSHKIN: But I didn't have it, you see, not even a word.

RADOMSKY: Do you know what I've been wondering, my poor dear Prince. I've been wondering whether you've ever really loved either of them?

MYSHKIN: What? What did you say? I - love them both - I - you're very clever - I know you're very clever - but I'm - I'm terribly sorry, my head has been aching again these last few days, I can't - I can't -

RADOMSKY: Then for God's sake, Prince - Men have behaved appallingly at times like this through out history- they've leapt on to horses and just galloped away from it all. And if anyone's entitled to a burst of bad behaviour - There, I've said it. Don't do it, Prince. Don't. Not for that woman! She's not worth it. Why she's a monster! Believe me, I know it. Don't do it!

MYSHKIN: I think you're trying to be very kind to me. But you see, if I don't she'll die. I know it.

(Looks at him, then suddenly, in a shaking voice.)

But the thing is, I'm afraid of her. Afraid. Her eyes - I can't bear to look into her eyes - she's mad - she's mad, you see.

RADOMSKY: Well, there you are - you can't love her - can you? You really can't.

MYSHKIN: I love her with all my heart!

(Exit RADOMSKY.

LEBEDEV enters, carrying a tray of drinks.)

LEBEDEV: A celebration refreshment, your Highness, to commemorate the occasion.

MYSHKIN: Why, thank you, thank you.

LEBEDEV: Well... happiness.

KELLER: Happiness... Well.

LEBEDEV: Well, Prince, there's something I have to tell you.

(GANYA enters.)

MYSHKIN: Ganya, my dear Ganya - I hoped you would come.

GANYA: I... I just wanted to wish you all happiness... personally ... I would have come before except I've um, been very busy.

LEBEDEV: Yes. Yes you have, haven't you? Why don't you tell the Prince what you've been busy at.

GANYA: I beg your pardon?

LEBEDEV: Who do you think's been Nastasya Filippovna's spy? Who do you think's been watching you for her? And all because he's after Miss Aglaya again.

GANYA: You're lying!

LEBEDEV: Am I? You see how it's worked out for him, Prince? He stopped Mr Radomsky marrying her and now you. But you won't get her. She doesn't want you... Judas!

GANYA: Judas - don't you dare call me Judas. This man, this faithful friend, has been trying to get you certified ever since your engagement - He's been to every doctor in Pavlovsk - even St Petersburg.

LEBEDEV: Yes, yes, I have, spy, because I love him, that's why.

GANYA: Do you think I don't love him. I love the Prince, just as much - more - more - I love him.

MYSHKIN: Please – this is my wedding. You are both my friends – I love you both.

(KELLER, who has come down, escorts MYSHKIN off. MYSHKIN first embraces LEBEDEV and GANYA, but IPPOLIT refuses his embrace.)

IPPOLIT: Well done, Prince, you've got two Judas's now. See what you do to people – You make Judas's of them.

GANYA: So you knew then? It doesn't matter now – it's too late now.

LEBEDEV: It's our natures, eh, just as he said. We can't help them. If we were all as good as him –

GANYA: What would become of us?

Scene Four

NASTASYA's wedding

VOICES OFF OF CROWD: Nastasya – Come on out – Nastasya Come on out – What are you afraid of, Nastasya? What are you afraid of, Nastasya? Come on and get married.

(NASTASYA enters, crosses down stage agitated. ROGO-ZHIN suddenly appears, crosses to NASTASYA.)

NASTASYA (relieved): Take me away from this – take me away, etc.

(ROGOZHIN picks her up in his arms, exits up stage.)

VOICES: Nastasya – Nastasya...

(In chant.)

FERDYSCHENKO: As it was in the beginning is now and ever shall be, a whore remains a whore. Thy will be done. Open the brothels, open the prisons. A glorious sinner is saved from salvation.

Scene Five

ROGOZHIN's room

Lights up. ROGOZHIN sitting by the bed, on a chair. The room is very dim but the candle under the Holbein lit. ROGOZHIN gets up, goes to the door.

ROGOZHIN: Come up, Prince, come up. I've been waiting.

(As MYSHKIN enters.)

I thought you'd be here before this, did you have to wait for the morning train –

(Leads him to a chair.)

– or did you hire a carriage, here, are you cold, sit down, make yourself comfortable. Tired eh? Are you?

MYSHKIN: Parfyon, where is she?

ROGOZHIN: She knew you'd come. Do you know, she was frightened of you? She kept making me promise to take her away. Did you know she was frightened? Why? You'd never harm her, would you?

(MYSHKIN puts his hand on the curtains, makes as if to draw them back.)

No, no, go on, go on.

(Nodding.

MYSHKIN draws the curtains. NASTASYA revealed, covered by a sheet, the remains of torn wedding dress are apparent, a trickle of blood drying from below her left breast.

Takes MYSHKIN's hand, leads him back to the chair, sits him on the mattress beside it.)

No – no, don't tremble, Leo Nikolaievich, you mustn't tremble, are you cold? But it's warm here, I've heard the flies buzzing, very warm, mm?

MYSHKIN: What are you going to do, Parfyon?

ROGOZHIN: Yes, I waited until she was asleep, you see, and then I took the knife and just slipped it in, it went in very gently – I've been watching ever since, keeping the flies off, we'll stay here together a little while, shall we? We've got to keep you warm, though, you're very cold –

(Gets up, gets a blanket.)

Come –

(Gently.)

– come lie down.

(Puts the blanket over him.)

You'll feel warm in a minute – Did you see – there was hardly any blood, but they find it out, eh, with their buzzing – eh? She was frightened, you see – Do you hear something?

MYSHKIN: No, there's nothing.

ROGOZHIN: Sssssh! Listen! I'll shut the door now you're –

(Sees the door is shut, comes back, sits down, wraps the blanket around himself again. There is a silence. MYSHKIN is watching him.)

We used to play cards, you see, in Pavlovsk – that's how we spent our evenings when she wasn't thinking about – well, sometimes she used to like my being with her...·playing cards for hours, together...

(After a silence.)

Do you remember, Nikolai, she threw the money into the fire, eh? Hah? She was a queen! She made him crawl – and the ear-rings, she threw them back in his face, eh! Eh!

(There is another silence.

Stiffening.)

Prince!

(Whispered urgently.)

Prince!

(Screamed.)

Leo Nikolai –

(Babbling.)

When she was... when she was...

(MYSHKIN pulls ROGOZHIN against him, strokes his head, stares out calmly, as ROGOZHIN continues to babble. The light is on the two of them, the rest is darkness, except for the illuminated Holbein behind.

As his body is slowly covered in darkness.)

I was on the train, coming back, coming back, ah, the little swine, she knew I'd be - I was - she waiting for me, waiting, because of the ear-rings, eh? If it hadn't been for the flies, buzzing, buzzing, Leo - ah Prince, Prince, I love...

(Going down to a whimper as the darkness comes over his face, resting in MYSHKIN's lap.

MYSHKIN is staring calmly ahead, cuddling ROGOZHIN's head as the darkness drifts up, until only his shoulders and head are distinct. Then he smiles. The smile dissolves into imbecility as the jaw drops, the gaze becomes vacant.

FERDYSCHENKO (walks slowly towards MYSHKIN, bends down, looks into his face): Prince? Prince?

(Very gently, enquiringly.)

Are you there? Eh?

(Takes MYSHKIN's jaw in his hand, tenderly, turns it about.)

Prince? Prince? Are you gone? All over is it, at last? All done, then? All done.

(FERDYSCHENKO nods, walks over to the Holbein, blows the candle out, then walks off stage, leaving MYSHKIN, with ROGOZHIN still in his arms.)

CURTAIN